# INTRODUCTION

The  is aimed at guitarists who are mystified by scales and modes. While there are many scale books available, a common roadblock is that most of these books just list every possible scale—useful or not—like a dictionary lists every word. With that method, it's easy to become intimidated and frustrated because your energy is spent trying to memorize scales and fingerings that you might not really need. Instead, you could be focusing on the important scales used most often by the masters. The  displays only the most essential scales that you'll need to have under your fingers in the most practical and useful fingerings, along with an easy-to-understand primer on how to create scales. Additionally, each of the scales presented is accompanied by a musical example on the included CD so you can actually hear what a specific scale or mode sounds like in a typical context.

While electric guitarists have created some of the most exciting music in history, the majority of them don't have the same command of scales as classical or jazz instrumentalists do because many guitarists learn from tabs or by rote—watching and imitating a peer or from watching a video. If you fall into that category and can already play your favorite songs, or if you already know some scales but want to expand your repertoire, the material in this book will add another dimension to your playing and writing. With a fundamental knowledge of the most common scales and a glimpse at how they're conventionally used, you'll soon be improvising your own solos or writing your own riffs without feeling like you're in the dark.

# ABOUT THE AUTHOR

New York City native Joe Charupakorn is a guitarist, editor, and best-selling author. He has written more than 20 instructional books for Hal Leonard Corporation including *Signature Licks: The Best of Yngwie Malmsteen*, *Signature Licks: Mike Stern*, *Jazz Improv Basics*, and *Classic Rock Heroes*. His books are available worldwide and have been translated into many languages. Visit him on the Web at joecharupakorn.com.

# ABOUT THE RECORDING

Guitars: Joe Charupakorn

Bass: Tom McGirr

Keyboards: Warren Wiegratz

Drums: Scott Schroedl

# ultimate Guitar®
## SCALE DECODER
### ESSENTIAL SCALES AND MODES FOR GUITAR

BY JOE CHARUPAKORN

ISBN 978-1-4584-1819-7

HAL•LEONARD®
CORPORATION
7777 W. BLUEMOUND RD. P.O. BOX 13819 MILWAUKEE, WI 53213

In Australia Contact:
**Hal Leonard Australia Pty. Ltd.**
4 Lentara Court
Cheltenham, Victoria, 3192 Australia
Email: ausadmin@halleonard.com.au

Visit Hal Leonard Online at
**www.halleonard.com**

# CONTENTS

# READING TAB

Tab is used for the actual musical examples and no reading of music notation is required to get the most out of this book. Here is an explanation of how to read tab if you're not already familiar.

Tablature graphically represents the guitar fingerboard. Each horizontal line represents a string, and each number represents a fret. Rhythmic values are shown using ovals, stems, and dots.

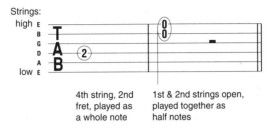

4th string, 2nd fret, played as a whole note

1st & 2nd strings open, played together as half notes

# THE CHROMATIC SCALE

A consists of every available note used in Western music. Here is the chromatic scale starting on C:

C C♯/D♭ D D♯/E♭ E F F♯/G♭ G G♯/A♭ A A♯/B♭ B C

In this spelling of the chromatic scale you'll notice that some notes have slashes and an alternate name. For example: C♯/D♭ or D♯/E♭. What that means is C♯ is the same note as D♭, and D♯ is the same note as E♭. Any note with an accidental—a sharp or flat—can be spelled either as a sharp or flat version of the note depending on its context. In this book, we'll list the most commonly encountered spellings but be aware that they are often interchangeable.

The chromatic scale can start on any note. Let's try it on the guitar. If you play every note on the 6th string starting from the open string and going up fret-by-fret to the 12th fret, you'll have played the chromatic scale from E to E. After the 12th fret, the chromatic scale starts over again.

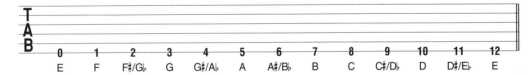

Let's try this on the 5th string. Here the chromatic scale is played starting on A. You should notice that other than the starting point, all of the chromatic scales we've looked at contain exactly the same notes.

# HALF STEPS AND WHOLE STEPS

and are terms used to describe the distance between two closely located notes. A half step is the distance from one note to the very next note. On the guitar, a half step is a one-fret distance. It doesn't matter whether you are going from one fretted note to another or from an open string to a fretted note or vice versa. It also doesn't matter whether one note is natural and the next one is also natural or has an accidental—sharp or flat. The actual distance is what we're measuring. For example: C to C#/Db is a half step, as is E to F.

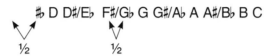

A whole step is a distance of two notes in the chromatic scale. On the guitar, this is a two-fret distance and as with half steps—or any interval for that matter—it doesn't matter whether one or both notes are fretted, or whether one note is natural and the other one is also natural or has an accidental. For example: D to E is a whole step as is A#/Bb to C.

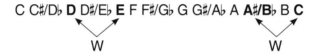

# CONSTRUCTING THE MAJOR SCALE

The —also referred to as the Ionian mode—is the foundation from which all the common scales and modes you'll hear in Western music are derived. To create a major scale, apply the following formula to the chromatic scale:

Whole–Whole–1/2– Whole–Whole–Whole–1/2

Starting on C we get:

Let's create a major scale starting on E and see how it relates to the guitar. This example is played exclusively on the 6th string.

**E Major Scale**

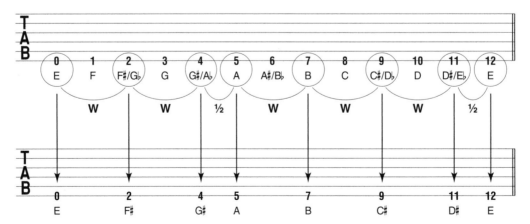

Here's the same idea starting on A, this time using the open 5th string of the guitar.

**A Major Scale**

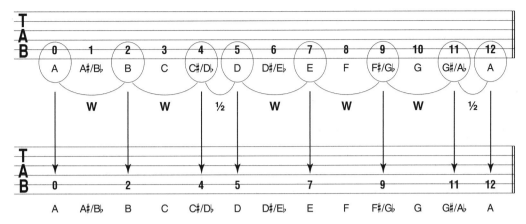

If you did this starting from every open string, you'll notice that all the major scales have exactly the same shape, in terms of fret location. This tells us that, other than the starting note, every major scale is exactly the same in terms of note relationships. Here's a C major scale played only on the 2nd string, starting from the 1st fret. Notice that the distance between the notes is exactly the same as the E and A major scales we just looked at.

**C Major Scale**

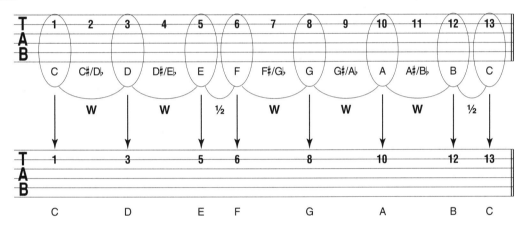

# PLAYING IN POSITION

The major scale fingerings we've looked at so far have been played on one string, but as you probably realize, most guitar music uses more than one string. There are countless ways to play the same notes using different combinations of strings so let's take a look at what the E major scale looks like in several different places on the guitar. Oftentimes, scales are played in position—meaning across several strings within a four-fret span and keeping a one-finger-per-fret fingering scheme.

Here's an E major scale fingering in the open position.

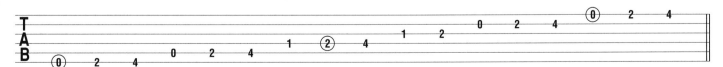

In this book, the fingerings shown will start at the lowest note in the position, which might not be the root of the scale. The root of the scale will always be indicated by a circle around the note throughout the book. In this next fingering, although the starting note is the 7th fret of the 6th string, the lowest root—as circled—is located on the 7th fret of the 5th string.

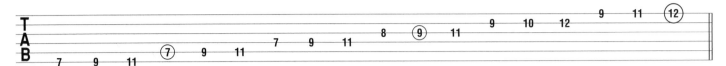

This fingering stretches out of position at the end.

There is no one "magic" fingering that works best for every case. The best choice really depends on the particular situation. You'll want to learn several different fingerings because some things will be easier to play from one scale fingering than another. This will change depending on context; a fingering that is comfortable to play fast may become uncomfortable for certain bends, like a first-finger bend. The more fingerings you learn, the more options you'll have at your disposal. But don't get caught in the trap of feeling like you have to master every single shape all over the neck before you start making music. You're better off memorizing two or three shapes that you can connect and easily visualize, then add other shapes later on, as the need arises.

The music comes first. Outside of a music school, no one is going to award you for your ability to play an E major scale all over the neck. What every person will notice is whether you sound good or not.

# MODES

Among guitarists, modes have been one of the most mythical and perplexing subjects of all time—bragging rights for those who understand them, complex-inducer for those who don't. A large part of the mystique comes from the fact that many electric guitarists are not formally trained, so anything with an academic bend can appear intimidating. In reality, the modes—while important—aren't really that big of a deal once you understand them. In fact, once you actually crack the code and understand how they work, you might think to yourself, "Is that all there is to it?"

In the simplest terms, a mode is a series of notes organized sequentially; beginning and ending on a given root. Although you'll hear some people debate this, modes are also scales. They work much the same way the major scale works. There are several ways to derive modes.

## Parent-Scale Approach

A mode contains the same notes as the parent scale but just starts and ends on a different note. If you took a major scale and started and ended on a note other than the tonic, you'll end up with a mode of that major scale. Here are the modes of C major:

| | | | | | | | | | | | | |
|---|---|---|---|---|---|---|---|---|---|---|---|---|
| C Major (Ionian) | C | D | E | F | G | A | B | C | | | | |
| D Dorian | | D | E | F | G | A | B | C | D | | | |
| E Phrygian | | | E | F | G | A | B | C | D | E | | |
| F Lydian | | | | F | G | A | B | C | D | E | F | |
| G Mixolydian | | | | | G | A | B | C | D | E | F | G |
| A Aeolian | | | | | | A | B | C | D | E | F | G | A |
| B Locrian | | | | | | | B | C | D | E | F | G | A | B |

Although the modes of the major scale have the same notes as the major scale that it's derived from, a mode will have a different root and thus a gravitational pull toward a different tonal center.

## The Parallel Method

The parallel method compares the notes of a mode against the major scale built from the same root. Comparing D Dorian against D Major, we see the difference is that D Dorian contains a b3 and a b7. This formula applies to every Dorian mode, regardless of the root.

| | | | | | | | | |
|---|---|---|---|---|---|---|---|---|
| D Dorian | | D | E | F | G | A | B | C | D |
| | | | | b3 | | | | b7 | |
| D Major | | D | E | F♯ | G | A | B | C♯ | D |

If we built major scales from the roots of all the modes we just looked at, the notes are spelled as:

| | | | | | | | | |
|---|---|---|---|---|---|---|---|---|
| D Major | D | E | F♯ | G | A | B | C♯ | D |
| E Major | E | F♯ | G♯ | A | B | C♯ | D♯ | E |
| F Major | F | G | A | B♭ | C | D | E | F |
| G Major | G | A | B | C | D | E | F♯ | G |
| A Major | A | B | C♯ | D | E | F♯ | G♯ | A |
| B Major | B | C♯ | D♯ | E | F♯ | G♯ | A♯ | B |

Here is a chart comparing all of the modes we looked at against the major scales from the same roots.

| D Dorian | D | E | F | G | A | B | C | D |
|---|---|---|---|---|---|---|---|---|
| | | | ♭3 | | | | ♭7 | |
| D Major | D | E | F♯ | G | A | B | C♯ | D |

| E Phrygian | E | F | G | A | B | C | D | E |
|---|---|---|---|---|---|---|---|---|
| | | ♭2 | ♭3 | | | ♭6 | ♭7 | |
| E Major | E | F♯ | G♯ | A | B | C♯ | D♯ | E |

| F Lydian | F | G | A | B | C | D | E | F |
|---|---|---|---|---|---|---|---|---|
| | | | | ♯4 | | | | |
| F Major | F | G | A | B♭ | C | D | E | F |

| G Mixolydian | G | A | B | C | D | E | F | G |
|---|---|---|---|---|---|---|---|---|
| | | | | | | | ♭7 | |
| G Major | G | A | B | C | D | E | F♯ | G |

| A Aeolian | A | B | C | D | E | F | G | A |
|---|---|---|---|---|---|---|---|---|
| | | | ♭3 | | | ♭6 | ♭7 | |
| A Major | A | B | C♯ | D | E | F♯ | G♯ | A |

| B Locrian | B | C | D | E | F | G | A | B |
|---|---|---|---|---|---|---|---|---|
| | | ♭2 | ♭3 | | ♭5 | ♭6 | ♭7 | |
| B Major | B | C♯ | D♯ | E | F♯ | G♯ | A♯ | B |

# STEP CONSTRUCTION

Modes can also be constructed using the step-pattern approach we looked at earlier. However, this approach is less commonly employed with modes. Here's the D Dorian mode in terms of step pattern.

D Dorian = W   ½   W   W   W   ½   W

Here's a chart of all of the modes of the major scale with the mode formulas and the step construction.

| Name | Formula | Step Pattern |
|---|---|---|
| Ionian (Major) | 1 2 3 4 5 6 7 | W W ½ W W W ½ |
| Dorian | 1 2 ♭3 4 5 6 ♭7 | W ½ W W W ½ W |
| Phrygian | 1 ♭2 ♭3 4 5 ♭6 ♭7 | ½ W W W ½ W W |
| Lydian | 1 2 3 ♯4 5 6 7 | W W W ½ W W ½ |
| Mixolydian | 1 2 3 4 5 6 ♭7 | W W ½ W W ½ W |
| Aeolian (Natural Minor) | 1 2 ♭3 4 5 ♭6 ♭7 | W ½ W W ½ W W |
| Locrian | 1 ♭2 ♭3 4 ♭5 ♭6 ♭7 | ½ W W ½ W W W |

Here's how the major scale and its modes overlap in terms of step patterns.

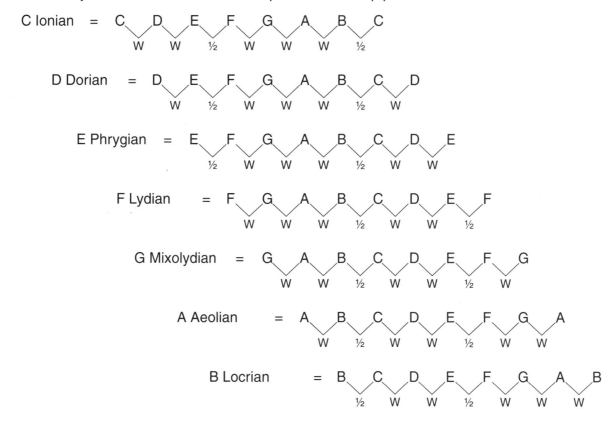

# CONSTRUCTING MINOR SCALES

A very loose definition of a minor scale is a scale that has a ♭3 contained within the notes. If you look at the formula chart you'll see that there are several scales and modes that fit that criteria—Dorian, Phrygian, Aeolian, and maybe Locrian (technically Locrian has a ♭5 so it's not officially a minor scale). The most common choice for a minor key is the natural minor scale, also known as the Aeolian mode, which contains the ♭3, ♭6, and ♭7.

You may hear the term used sometimes. That just means the minor scale that modally corresponds to a major scale. For example, A minor is the relative minor of C major because they both share the same notes, although they start and end in different places.

| A Natural Minor | A | B | C | D | E | F | G | A | | |
|---|---|---|---|---|---|---|---|---|---|---|
| C Major | | | C | D | E | F | G | A | B | C |

The other minor scale forms that you might come across are melodic minor and harmonic minor. We won't go into great detail on these two scales in this book but the formulas are:

Melodic Minor = ♭3

Harmonic Minor = ♭3, ♭6

Depending on how you think about it, there are countless ways to relate these or any scales and modes to something familiar. As we saw earlier, a natural minor scale is a major scale with a ♭3, ♭6, and ♭7. You could also say a natural minor scale is a Dorian mode with a ♭6 or a Phrygian mode with a ♮2. The possibilities are endless but I would suggest not getting carried away trying to figure out different ways to look at the same thing. Comparing scales and modes to the major scale and in some cases, the natural minor, will give you what you need. Otherwise, you'll soon hit the point of diminishing returns. For example, we all know that one dollar is equal to four quarters, ten dimes, twenty nickels, or a hundred pennies. That's probably all you really need to have committed to memory and from there you can compute any variants if need be. Going out of your way to memorize that one dollar is also three quarters plus two dimes plus five pennies, or forty-five pennies, a nickel, and two quarters becomes wasted energy very quickly.

# CONSTRUCTING PENTATONIC SCALES

For most rock guitar, the  is where it all begins. Pentatonic scales contain only five notes and are simpler than the major scale or its modes. A major pentatonic can be looked at as a major scale without the 4th or 7th. The formula is: 1, 2, 3, 5, 6. Here's E major in comparison with E major pentatonic. This is displayed on the 6th string for easier visualization.

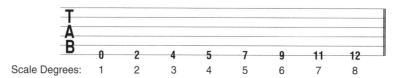

The minor pentatonic scale is by far the first choice for most rock guitar solos.

A minor pentatonic scale can be looked at as a natural minor scale, Dorian mode, or Phrygian mode, without the 2nd or 6th. The formula is: 1, ♭3, 4, 5, ♭7. Here's E natural minor in comparison with E minor pentatonic. This is displayed on the 6th string for easier visualization.

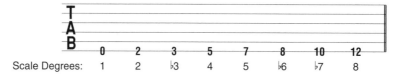

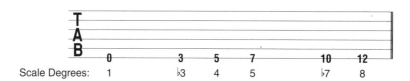

The minor and major pentatonic fingerings shown in this book are five moveable shapes that overlap and link to one another. If you memorize all five shapes you will be able to play anywhere on the neck and remain in key.

# CONSTRUCTING BLUES SCALES

A blues scale adds a ♯4 or ♭5 to a minor pentatonic scale. Here's an E minor pentatonic scale in comparison with E blues. This is displayed on the 6th string for easier visualization.

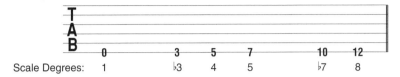

Scale Degrees:  1    ♭3   4    5    ♭7   8

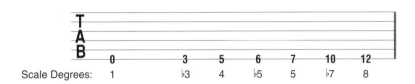

Scale Degrees:  1    ♭3   4    ♭5   5    ♭7   8

This extra note adds a distinctly bluesy sound. The opening riff to Cream's, "Sunshine of Your Love," is a prime example of what a blues scale sounds like.

# BEYOND THE BOX

In this book, we cover the scales most commonly used by electric guitarists: major scale and its modes, minor pentatonic, blues, and major pentatonic. Of course, there are many more scales out there that you'll hear in more harmonically involved styles like jazz, fusion, or prog-rock. Here's a list of formulas for some additional scales for you to experiment with.

| Name | Formula | Step Pattern |
|------|---------|--------------|
| Harmonic Minor | 1 2 ♭3 4 5 ♭6 7 | W ½ W W ½ W+½ ½ |
| Melodic Minor | 1 2 ♭3 4 5 6 7 | W ½ W W W W ½ |
| Dorian ♭2 | 1 ♭2 ♭3 4 5 6 ♭7 | ½ W W W W ½ W |
| Lydian Augmented | 1 2 3 ♯4 ♯5 6 7 | W W W W ½ W ½ |
| Lydian ♭7 | 1 2 3 ♯4 5 6 ♭7 | W W W ½ W ½ W |
| Mixolydian ♭6 (Hindu) | 1 2 3 4 5 ♭6 ♭7 | W W ½ W ½ W W |
| Locrian ♮2 | 1 2 ♭3 4 ♭5 ♭6 ♭7 | W ½ W ½ W W W |
| Super Locrian | 1 ♭2 ♭3 ♭4 ♭5 ♭6 ♭7 | ½ W ½ W W W W |
| Whole Tone | 1 2 3 ♯4 ♯5 ♭7 | W W W W W W |
| Diminished-half/whole | 1 ♭2 ♯2 3 ♯4 5 6 ♭7 | ½ W ½ W ½ W ½ W |
| Diminished-whole/half | 1 2 ♭3 4 ♯4 ♯5 6 7 | W ½ W ½ W ½ W ½ |

On pages 134–136 are fingerings for several scales commonly heard outside of rock including the harmonic and melodic minor as well as some of their modes, and symmetrical scales like: the whole tone, diminished-half/whole, and diminished-whole/half scales. You can hear these scales used by exciting players such as Yngwie Malmsteen, Steve Vai, Mike Stern, Scott Henderson, John Scofield, and Allan Holdsworth.

# E MAJOR (IONIAN)

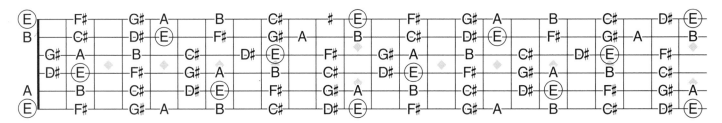

E F# G# A B C# D#          1 2 3 4 5 6 7

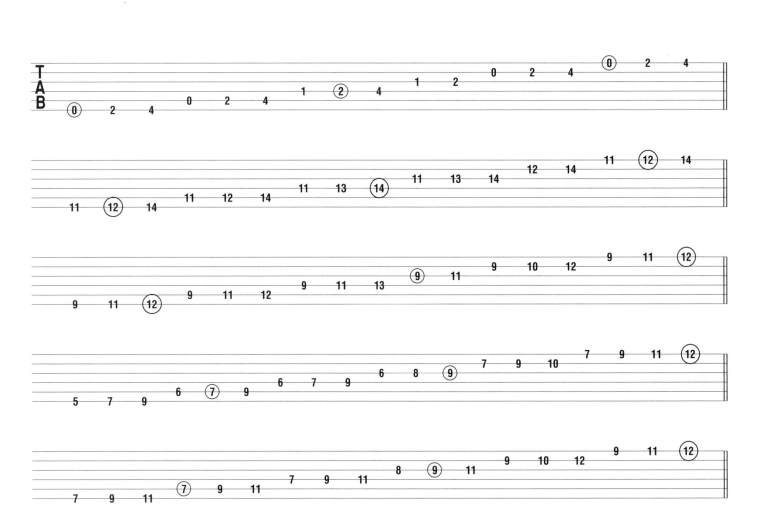

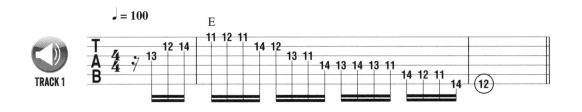

TRACK 1

# F MAJOR (IONIAN)

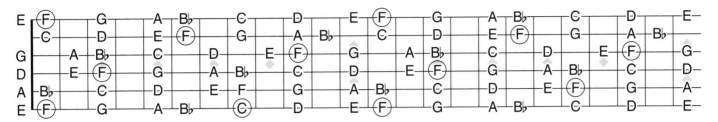

F G A B♭ C D E          1 2 3 4 5 6 7

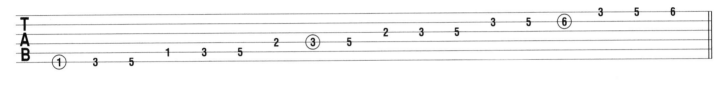

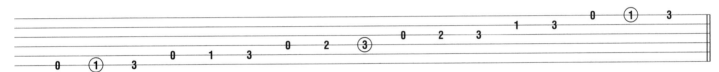

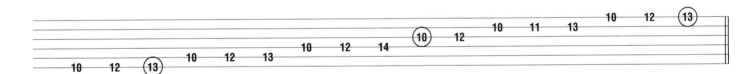

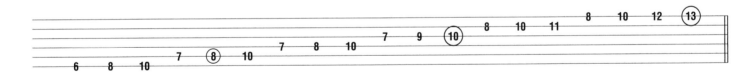

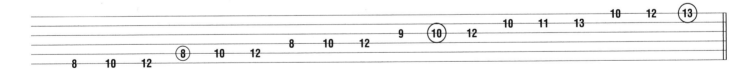

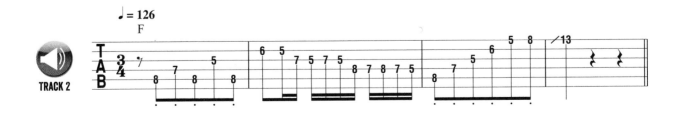

TRACK 2

# F#/Gb MAJOR (IONIAN)

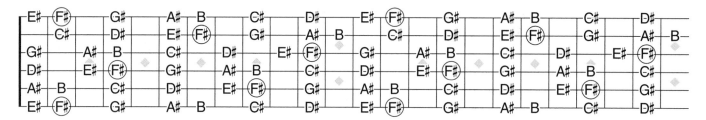

F# G# A# B C# D# E#          1 2 3 4 5 6 7

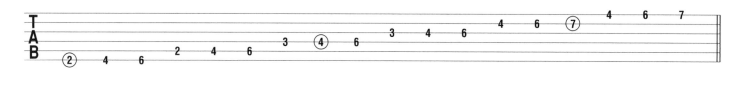

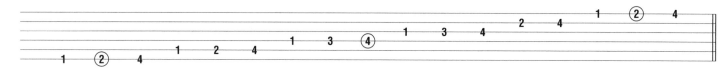

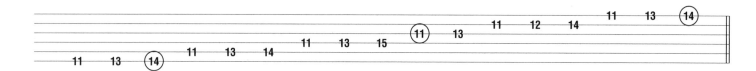

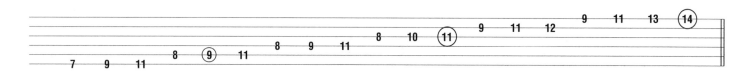

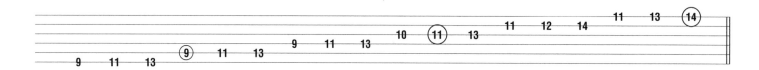

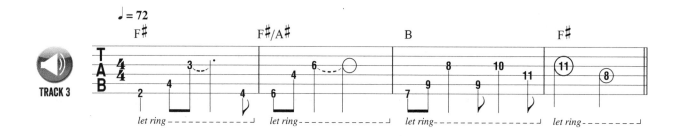

# G MAJOR (IONIAN)

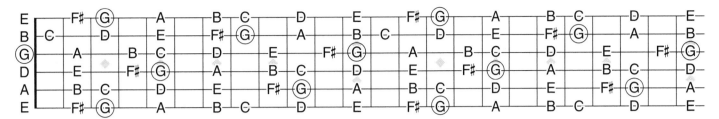

G A B C D E F#          1 2 3 4 5 6 7

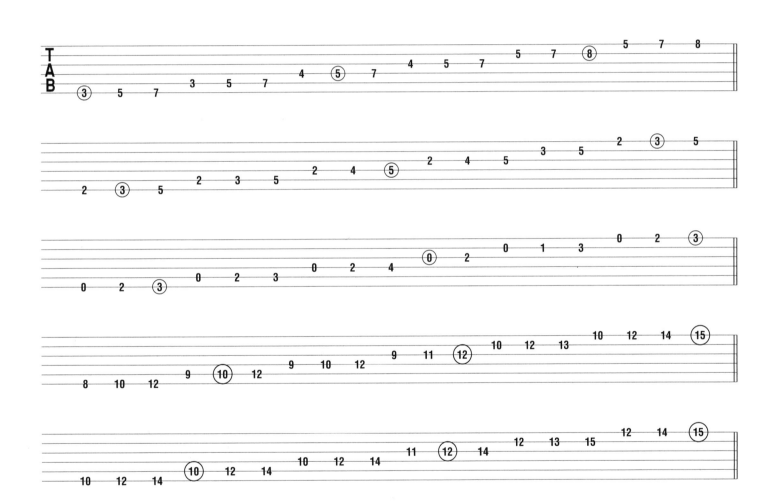

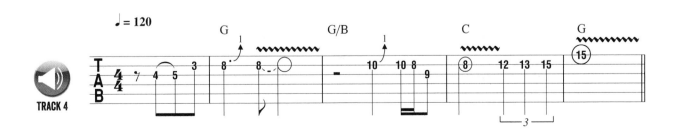

# G#/Ab MAJOR (IONIAN)

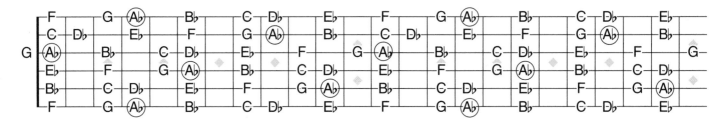

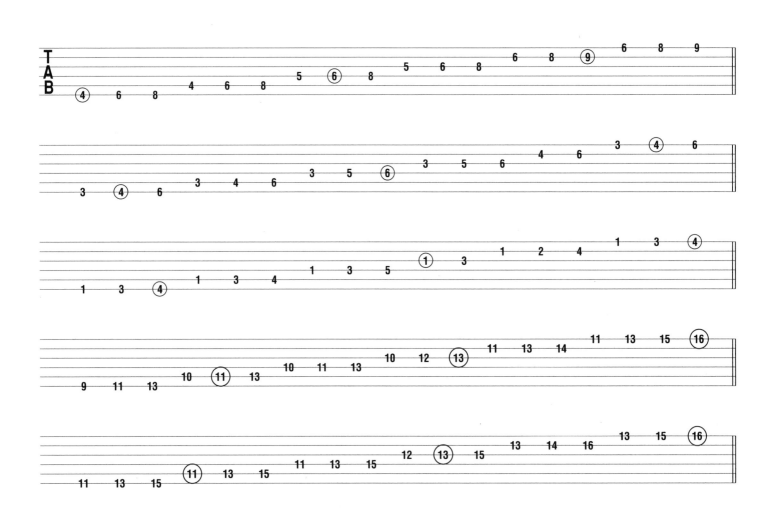

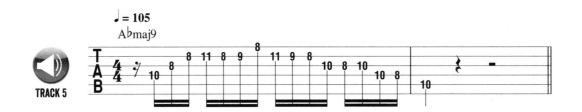

# A MAJOR (IONIAN)

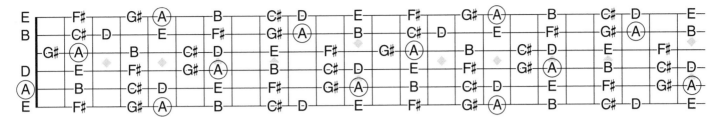

A B C# D E F# G#        1 2 3 4 5 6 7

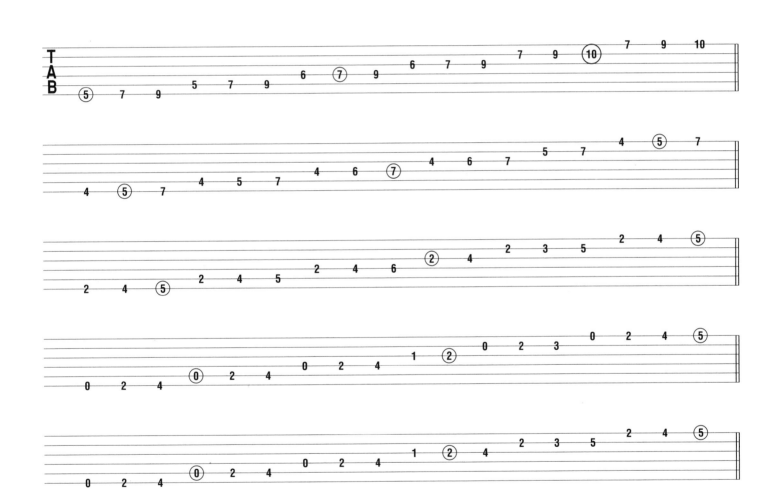

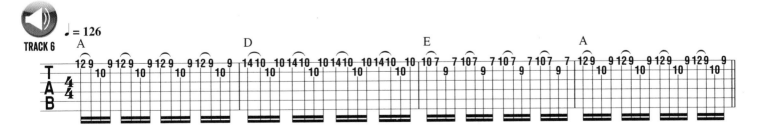

TRACK 6

♩ = 126

# A#/B♭ MAJOR (IONIAN)

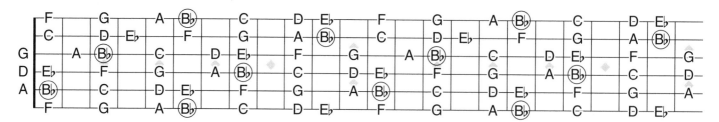

B♭ C D E♭ F G A          1 2 3 4 5 6 7

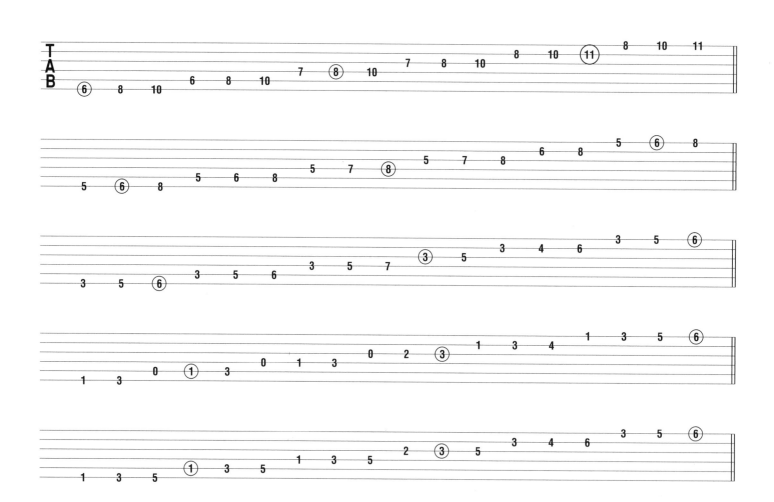

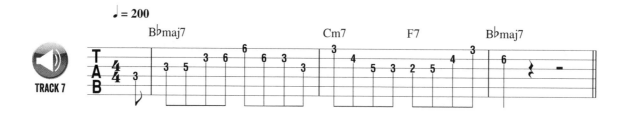

# B MAJOR (IONIAN)

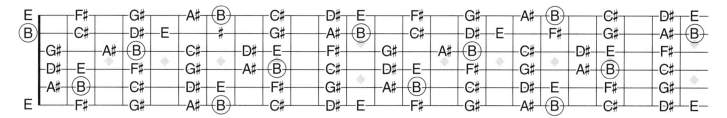

B C# D# E F# G# A#          1 2 3 4 5 6 7

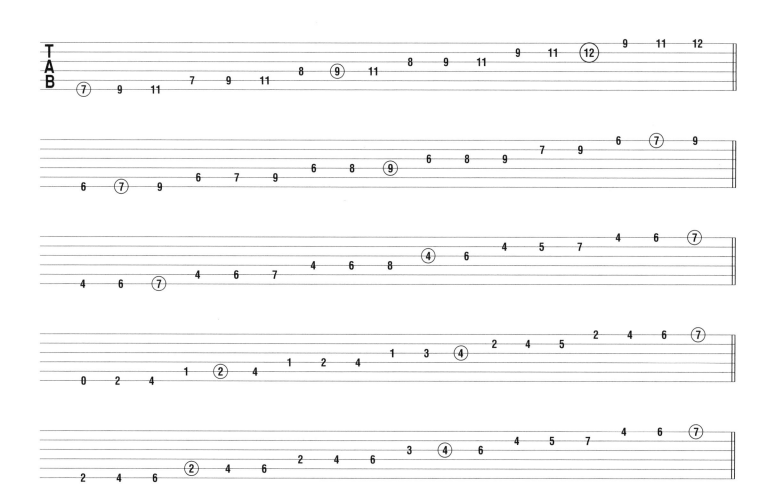

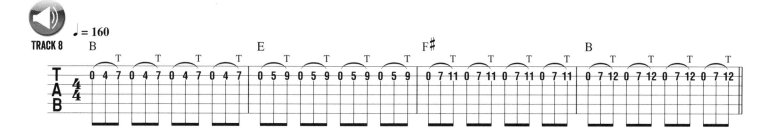

TRACK 8

# C MAJOR (IONIAN)

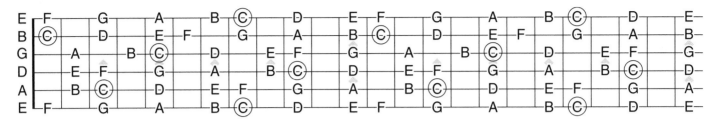

C D E F G A B     1 2 3 4 5 6 7

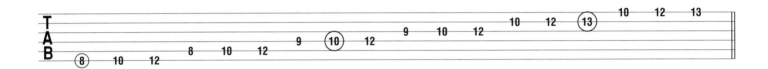

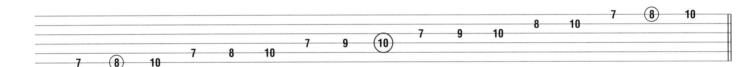

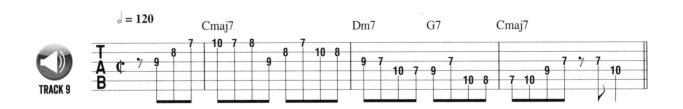

# C#/Db MAJOR (IONIAN)

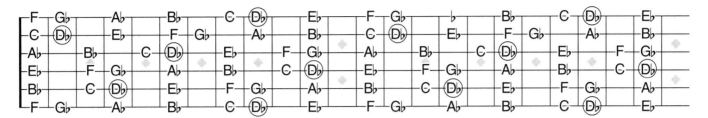

Db Eb F Gb Ab Bb C       1 2 3 4 5 6 7

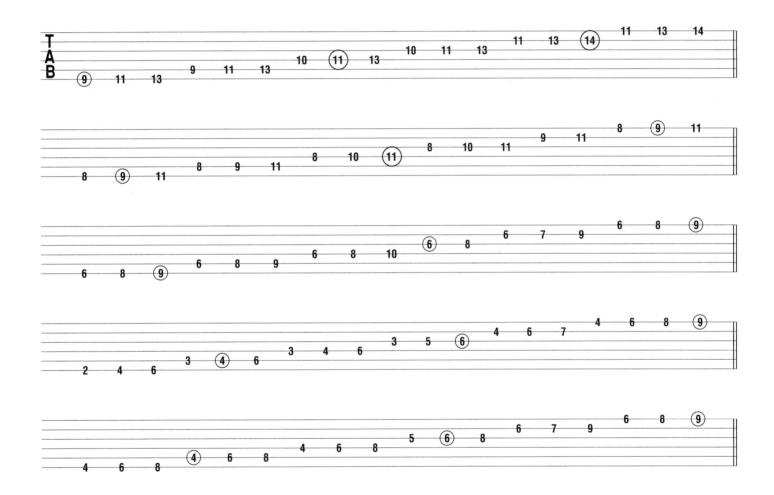

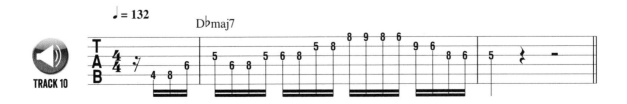

# D MAJOR (IONIAN)

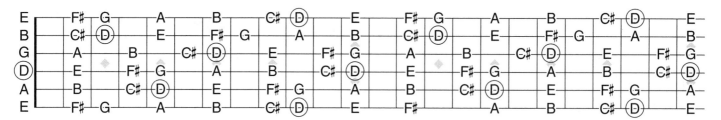

D E F# G A B C#          1 2 3 4 5 6 7

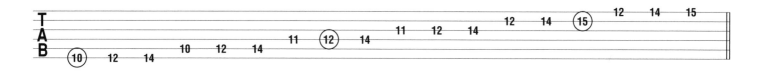

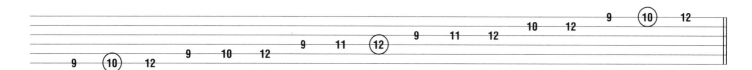

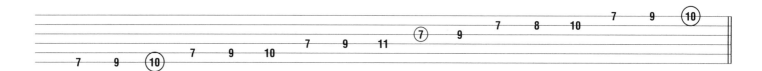

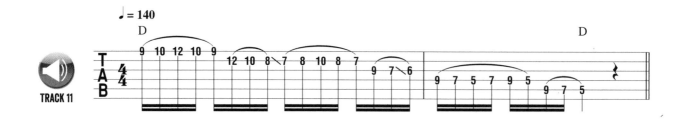

TRACK 11

# D#/E♭ MAJOR (IONIAN)

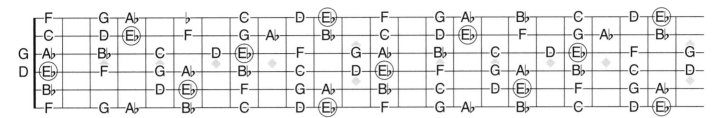

E♭ F G A♭ B♭ C D          1 2 3 4 5 6 7

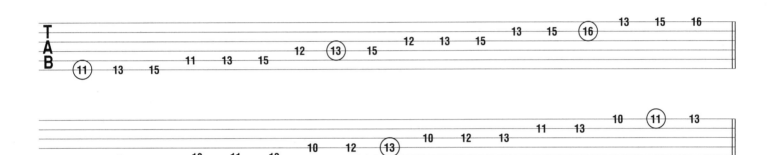

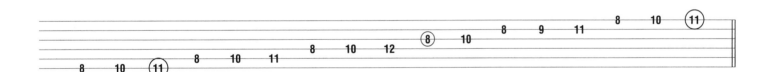

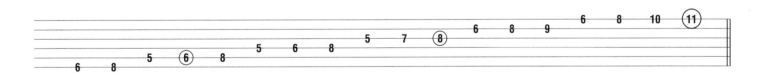

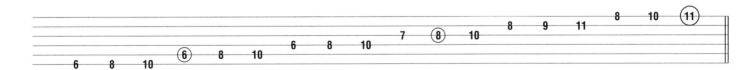

TRACK 12    ♩ = 115

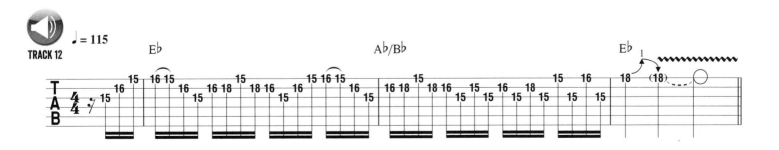

# E DORIAN

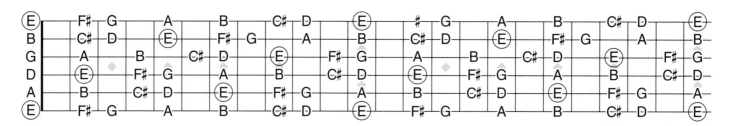

E F# G A B C# D          1 2 ♭3 4 5 6 ♭7

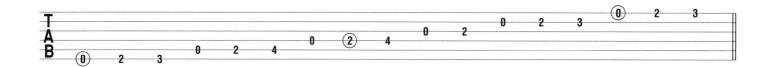

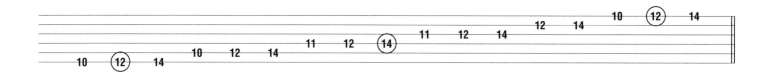

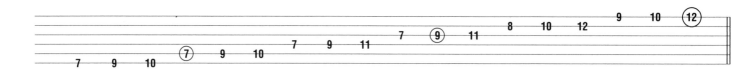

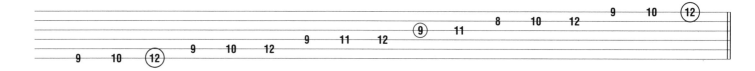

**TRACK 13**  ♩ = 90

Em7

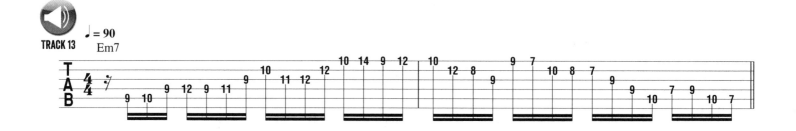

# F DORIAN

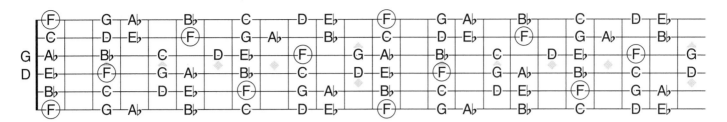

F G A♭ B♭ C D E♭          1 2 ♭3 4 5 6 ♭7

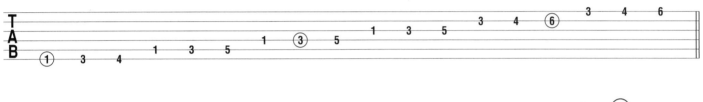

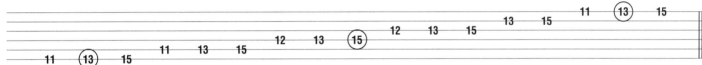

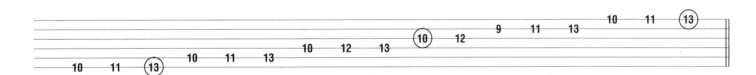

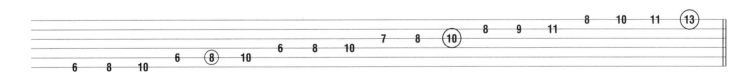

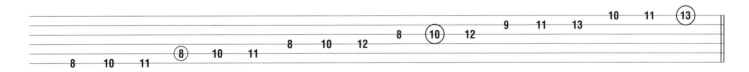

♩ = 100

TRACK 14

Fm7

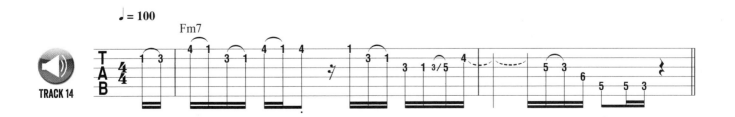

# F#/Gb DORIAN

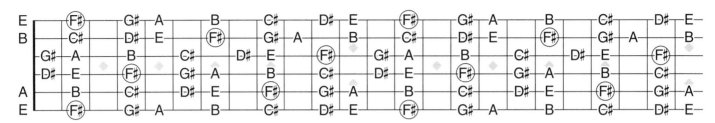

F# G# A B C# D# E        1 2 b3 4 5 6 b7

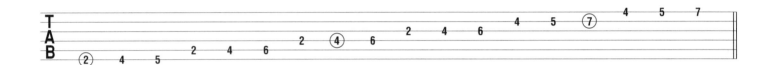

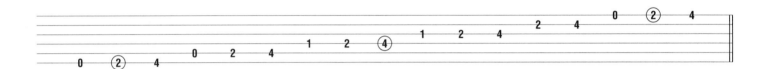

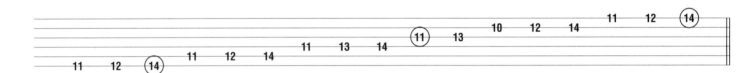

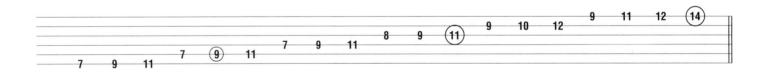

♩ = 110

**TRACK 15** F#m7

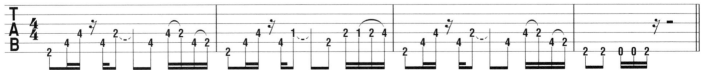

# G DORIAN

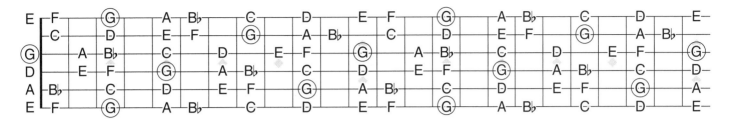

G A B♭ C D E F          1 2 ♭3 4 5 6 ♭7

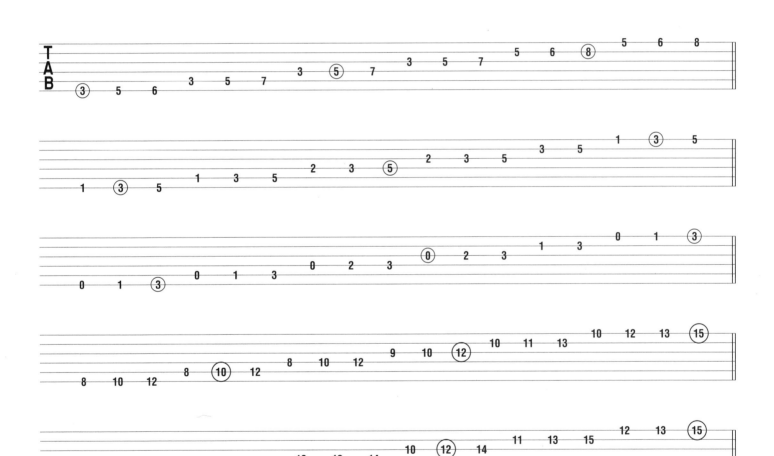

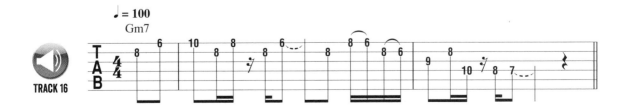

TRACK 16

# G#/A♭ DORIAN

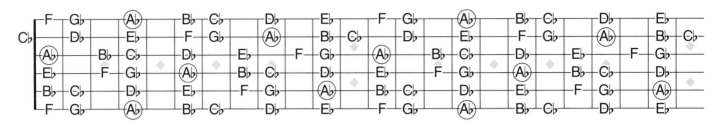

A♭ B♭ C♭ D♭ E♭ F G♭          1 2 ♭3 4 5 6 ♭7

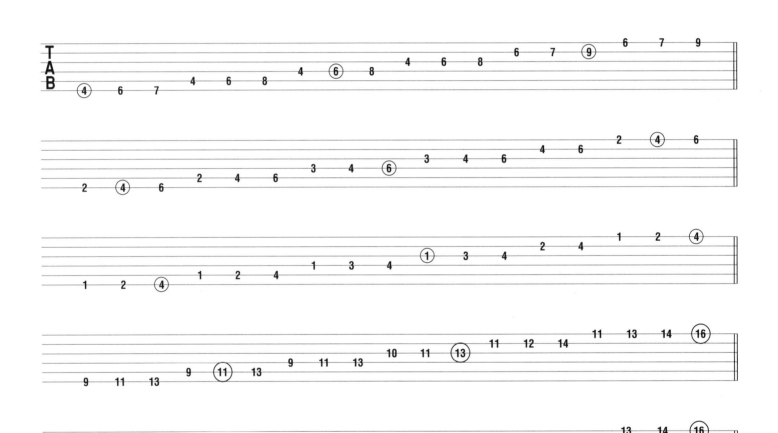

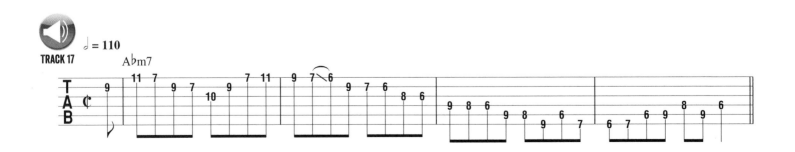

# A DORIAN

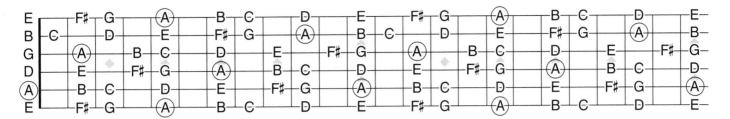

A B C D E F♯ G      1 2 ♭3 4 5 6 ♭7

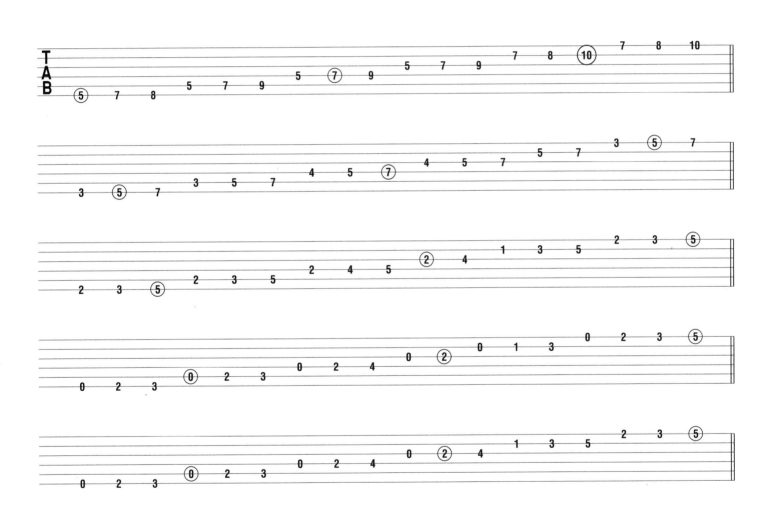

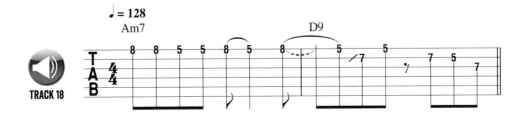

TRACK 18

# A#/Bb DORIAN

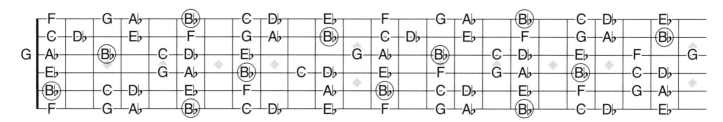

Bb C Db Eb F G Ab          1 2 b3 4 5 6 b7

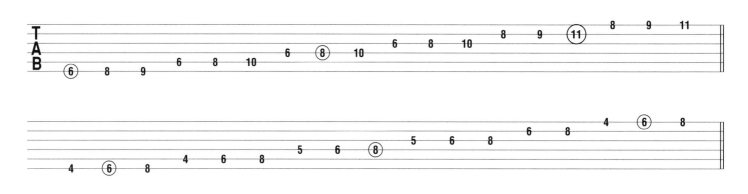

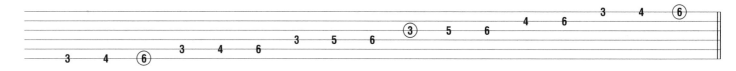

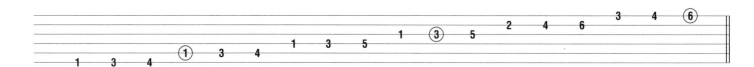

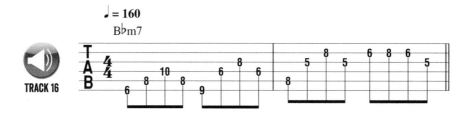

# B DORIAN

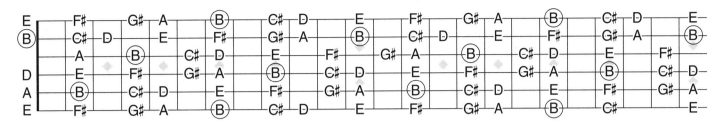

B C# D E F# G# A     1 2 ♭3 4 5 6 ♭7

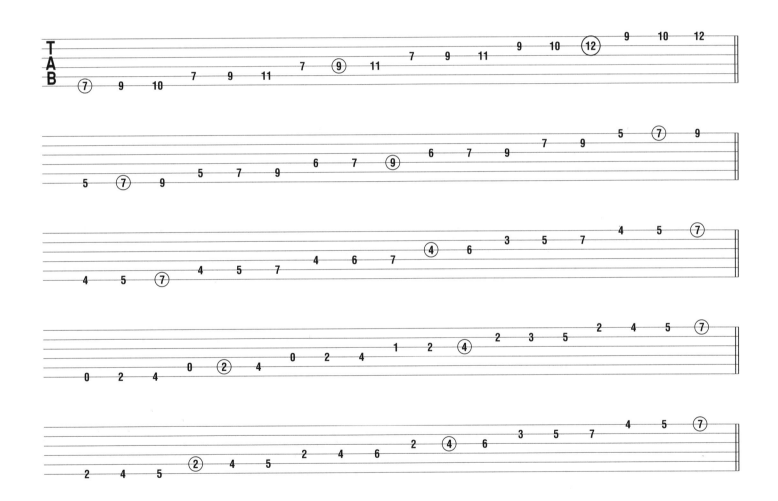

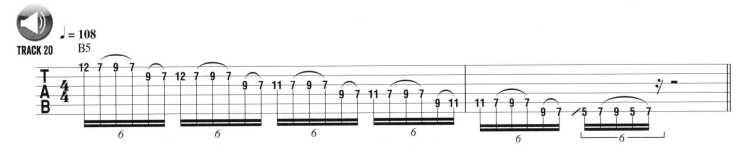

TRACK 20

♩ = 108
B5

# C DORIAN

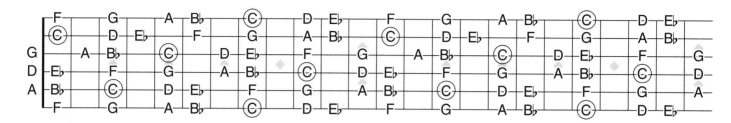

C D E♭ F G A B♭          1 2 ♭3 4 5 6 ♭7

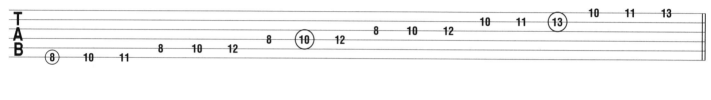

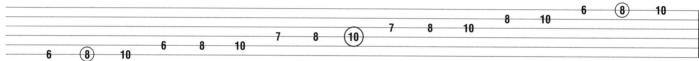

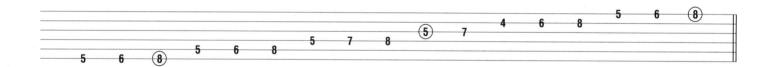

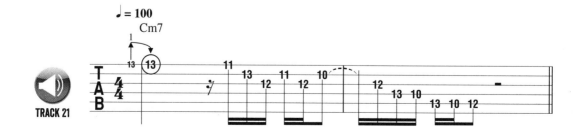

# C#/D♭ DORIAN

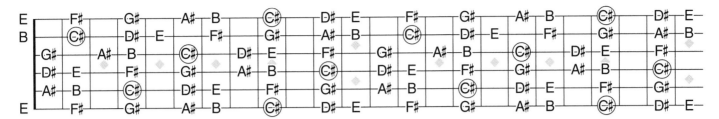

C# D# E F# G# A# B    1 2 ♭3 4 5 6 ♭7

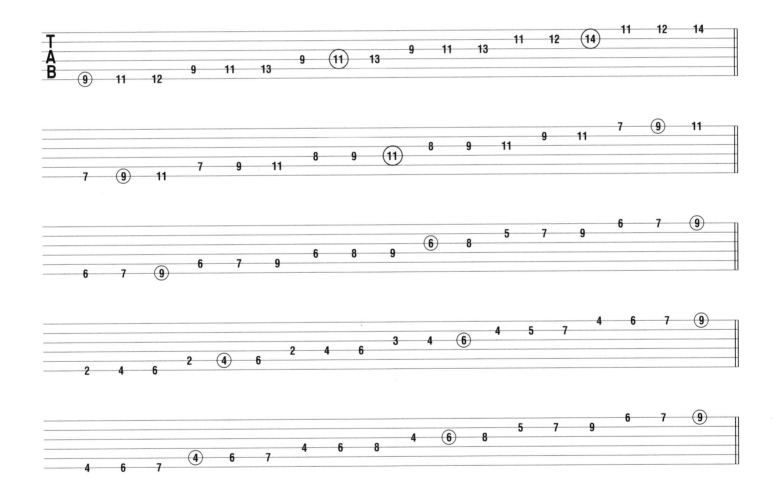

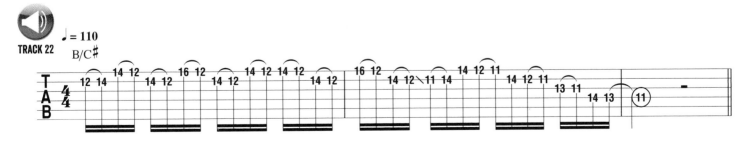

# D DORIAN

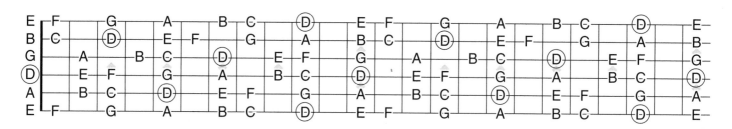

D E F G A B C      1 2 ♭3 4 5 6 ♭7

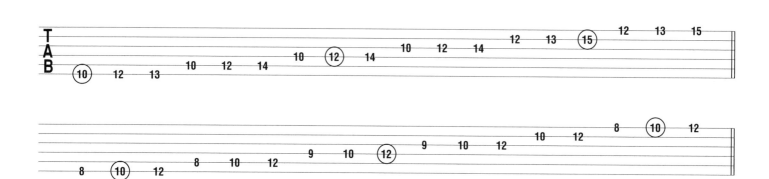

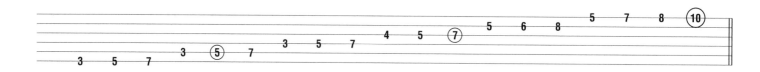

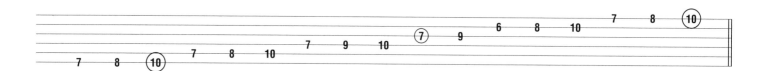

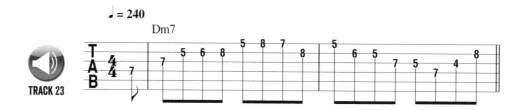

TRACK 23

# D#/Eb DORIAN

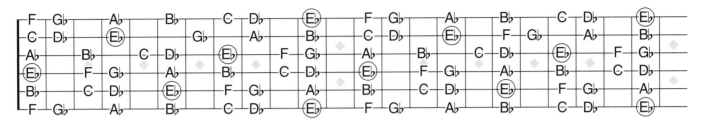

Eb F Gb Ab Bb C Db        1 2 b3 4 5 6 b7

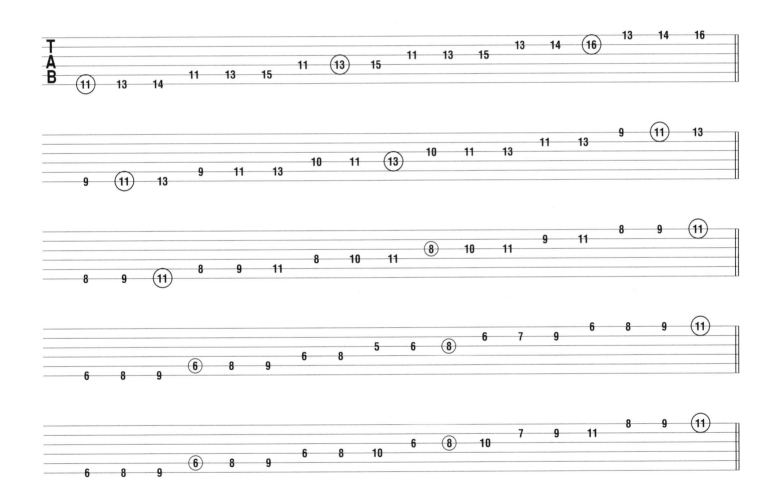

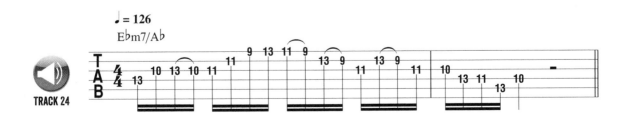

# E PHRYGIAN

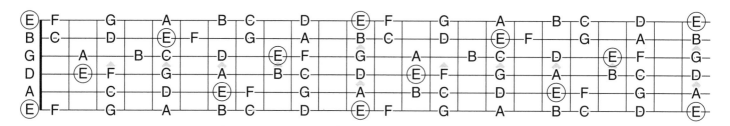

E F G A B C D        1 ♭2 ♭3 4 5 ♭6 ♭7

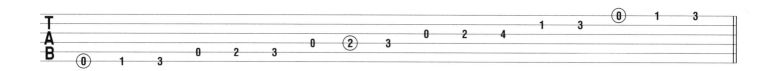

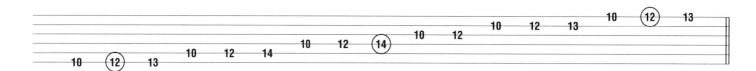

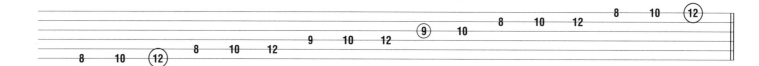

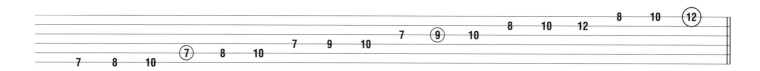

TRACK 25

♩ = 104

Fmaj7♯11/E

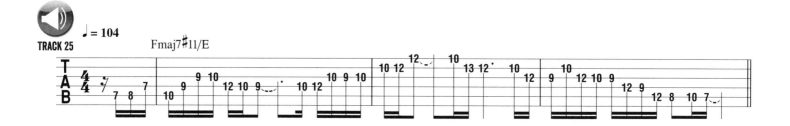

# F PHRYGIAN

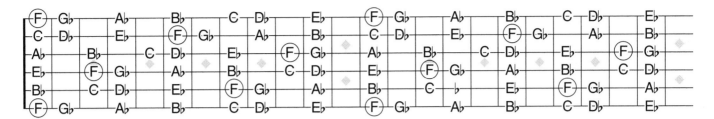

F Gb Ab Bb C Db Eb       1 b2 b3 4 5 b6 b7

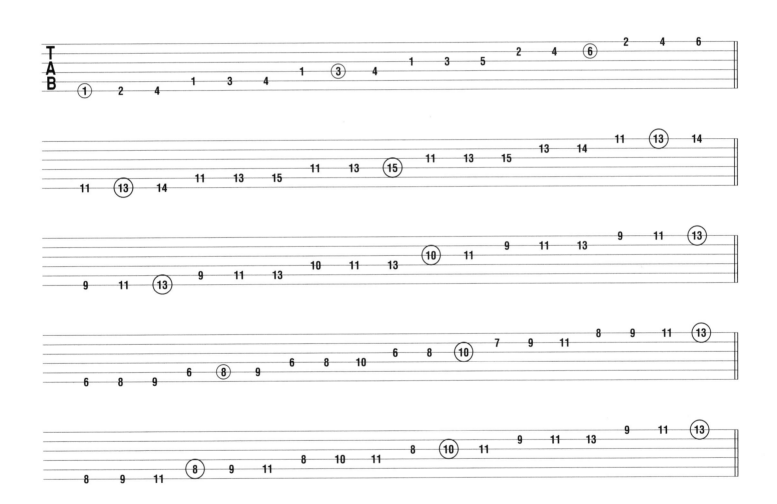

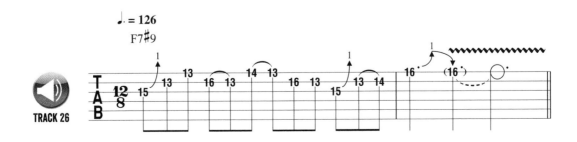

# F#/Gb PHRYGIAN

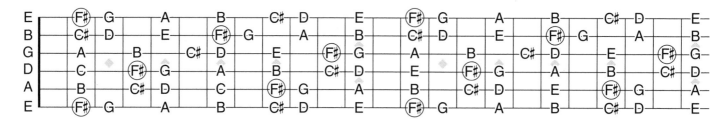

F# G A B C# D E          1 b2 b3 4 5 b6 b7

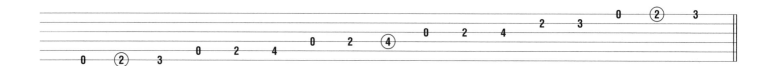

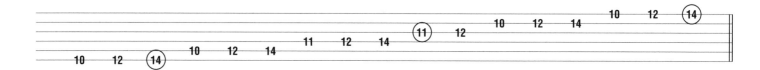

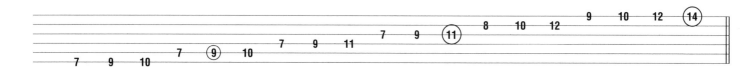

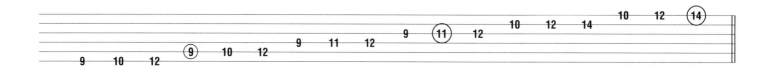

**TRACK 27**  ♩ = 120  F#7susb9

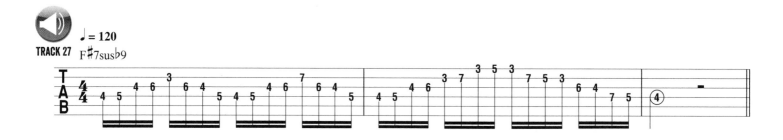

# G PHRYGIAN

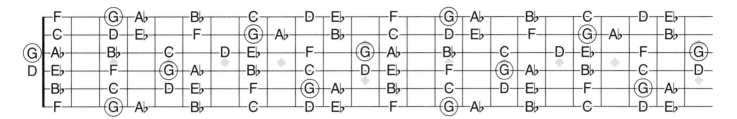

G Ab Bb C D Eb F     1 b2 b3 4 5 b6 b7

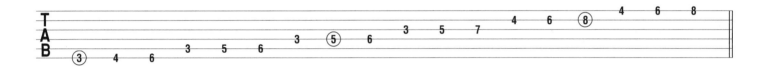

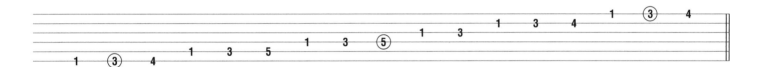

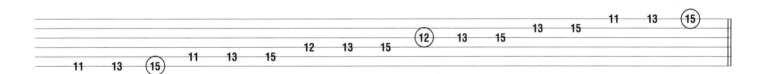

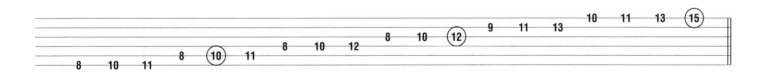

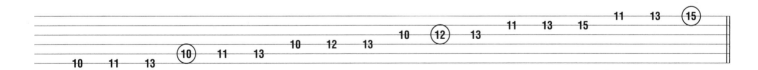

= 120

Ab/G

TRACK 28

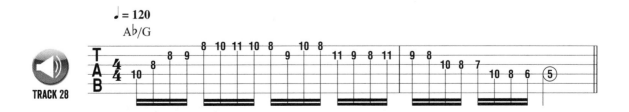

# G♯/A♭ PHRYGIAN

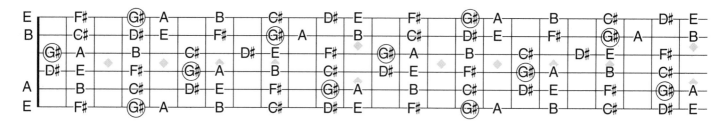

G♯ A B C♯ D♯ E F♯          1 ♭2 ♭3 4 5 ♭6 ♭7

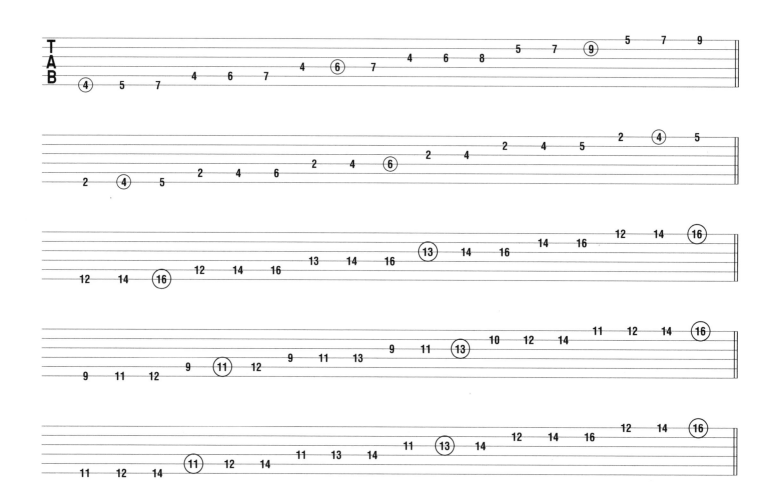

♩ = 120

Amaj7♯11/G♯

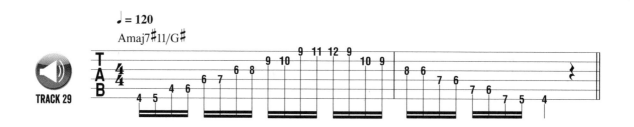

TRACK 29

# A PHRYGIAN

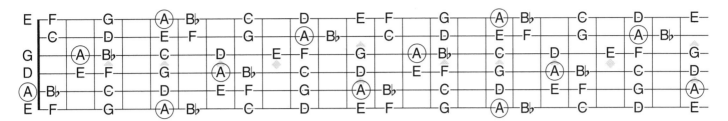

A B♭ C D E F G      1 ♭2 ♭3 4 5 ♭6 ♭7

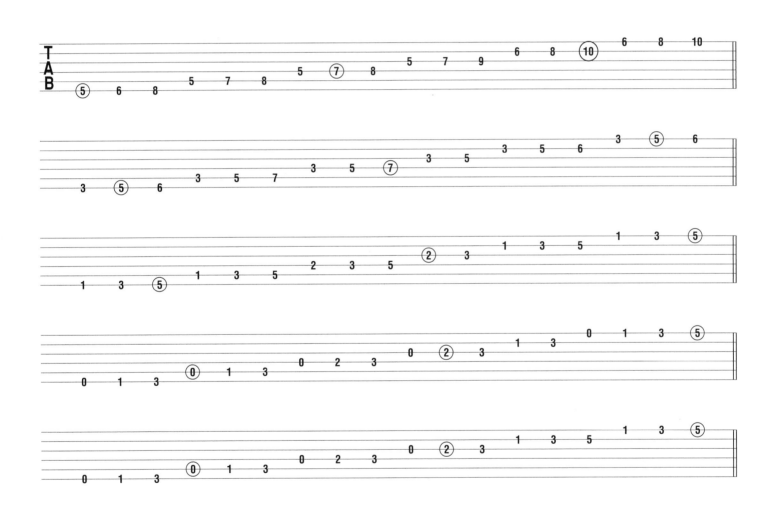

♩ = 126

B♭/A

TRACK 30

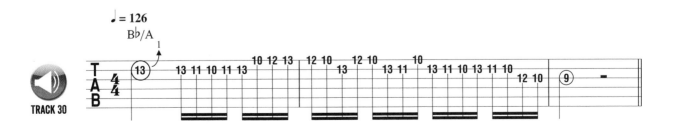

# A#/Bb PHRYGIAN

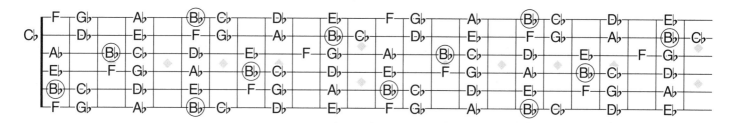

Bb Cb Db Eb F Gb Ab          1 b2 b3 4 5 b6 b7

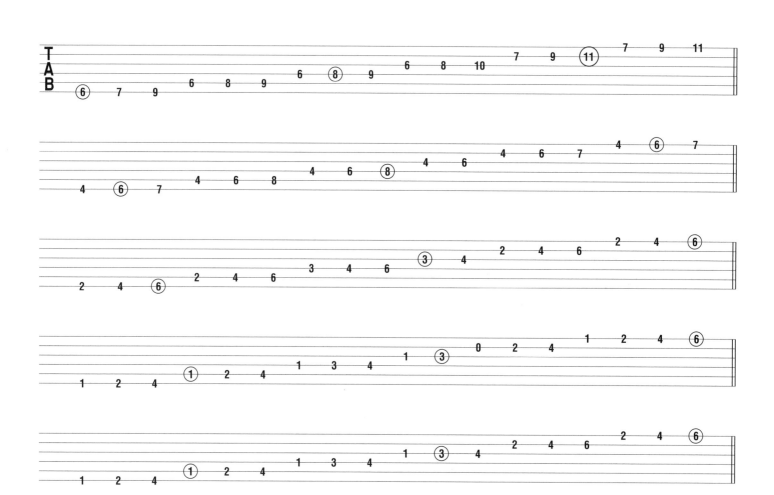

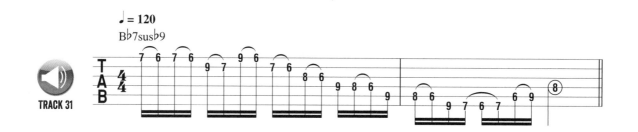

# B PHRYGIAN

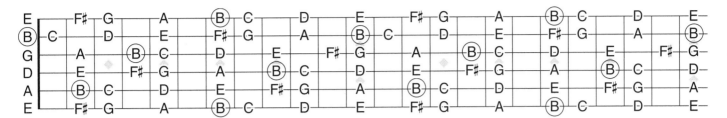

B C D E F# G A          1 ♭2 ♭3 4 5 ♭6 ♭7

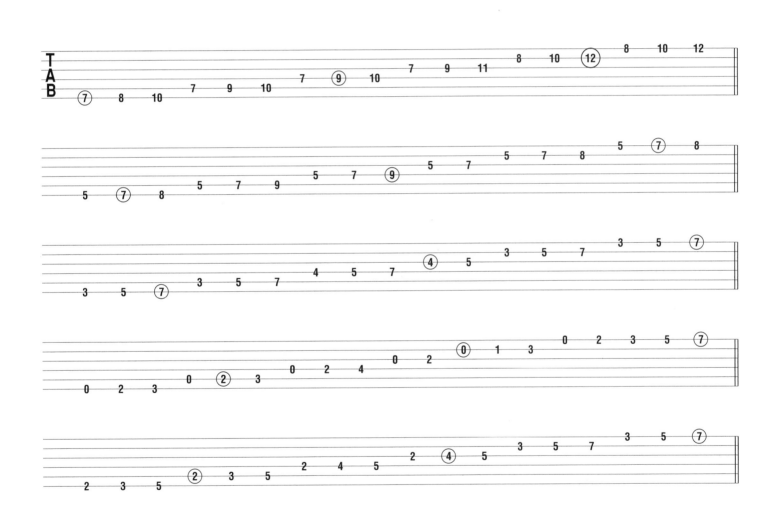

🔊 ♩ = 104

**TRACK 32**  Cmaj7#11/B

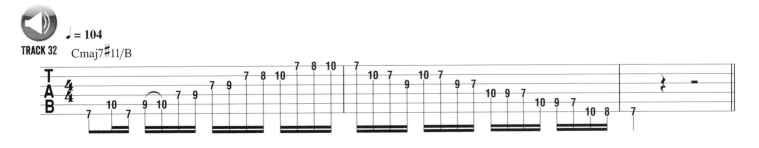

# C PHRYGIAN

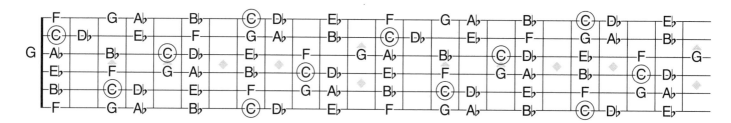

C Db Eb F G Ab Bb          1 b2 b3 4 5 b6 b7

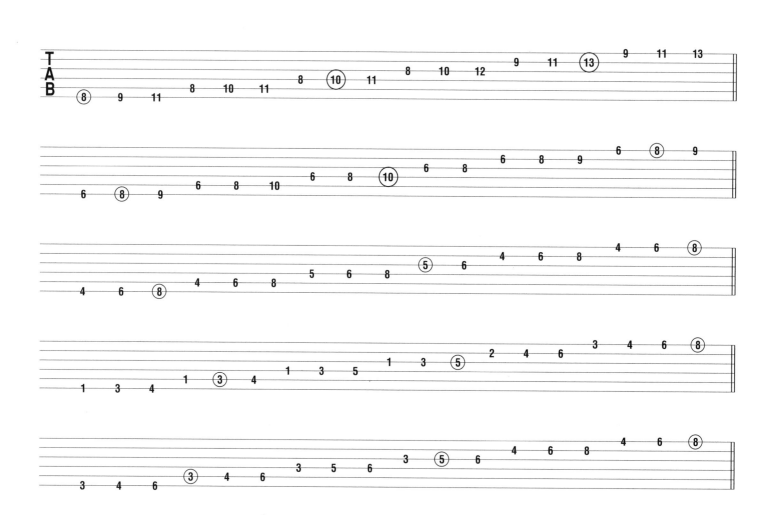

♩ = 126

Db/C

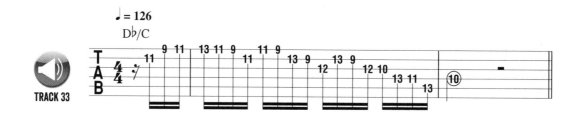

TRACK 33

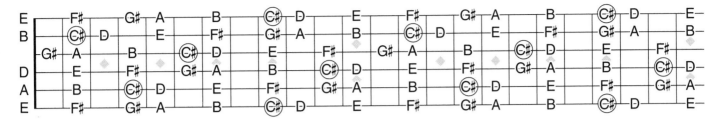

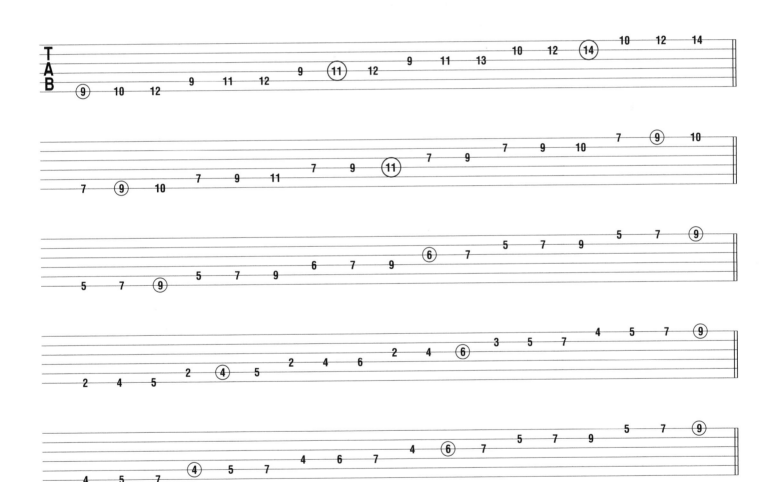

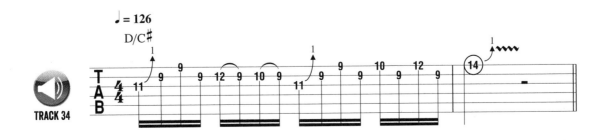

# C#/Db PHRYGIAN

C# D E F# G# A B    1 b2 b3 4 5 b6 b7

# D PHRYGIAN

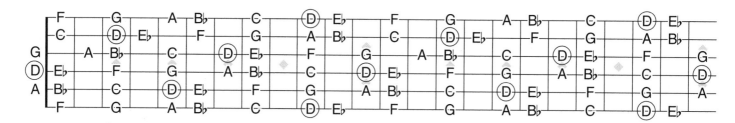

D E♭ F G A B♭ C          1 ♭2 ♭3 4 5 ♭6 ♭7

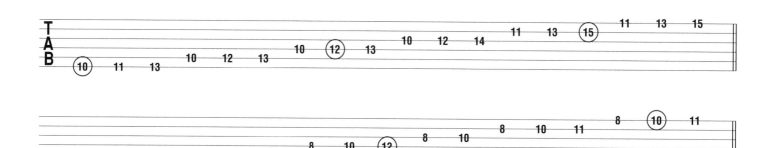

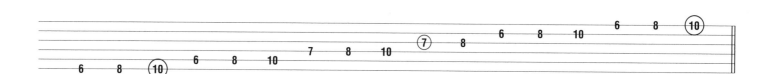

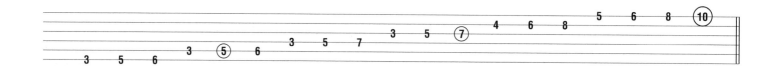

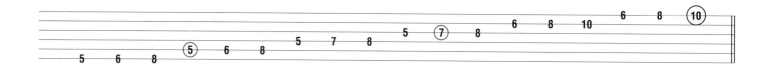

TRACK 35    ♩ = 132

E♭/D

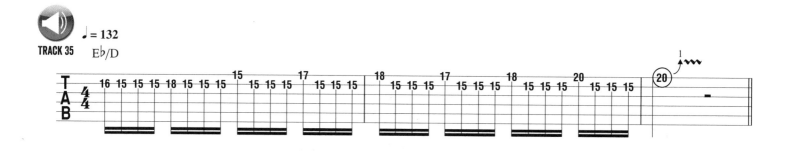

# D#/E♭ PHRYGIAN

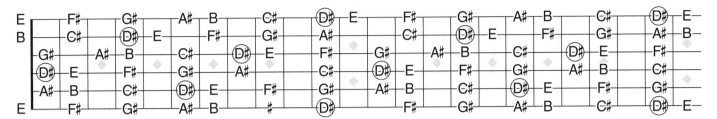

D# E F# G# A# B C#    1 ♭2 ♭3 4 5 ♭6 ♭7

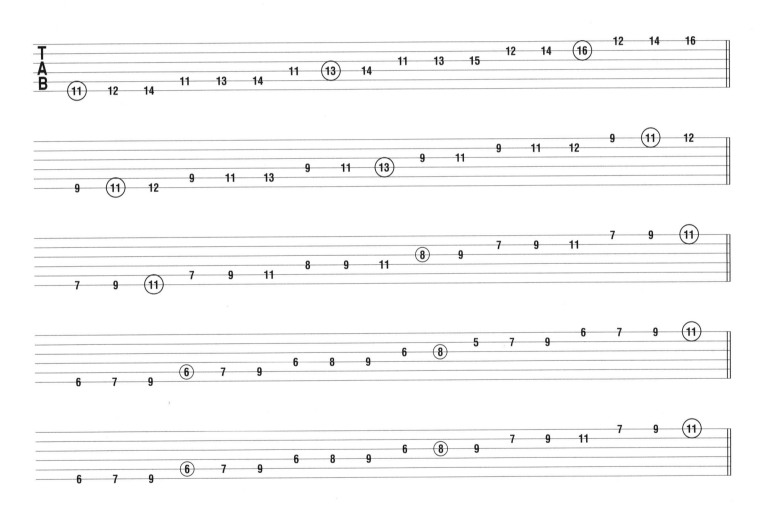

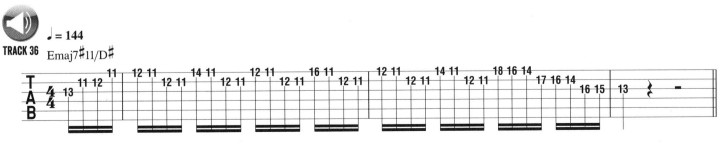

TRACK 36　Emaj7#11/D#　♩ = 144

49

# E LYDIAN

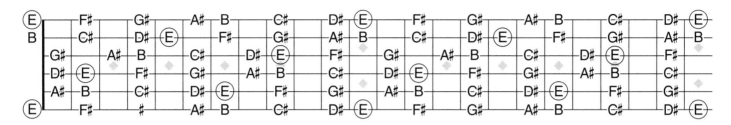

E F# G# A# B C# D#        1 2 3 #4 5 6 7

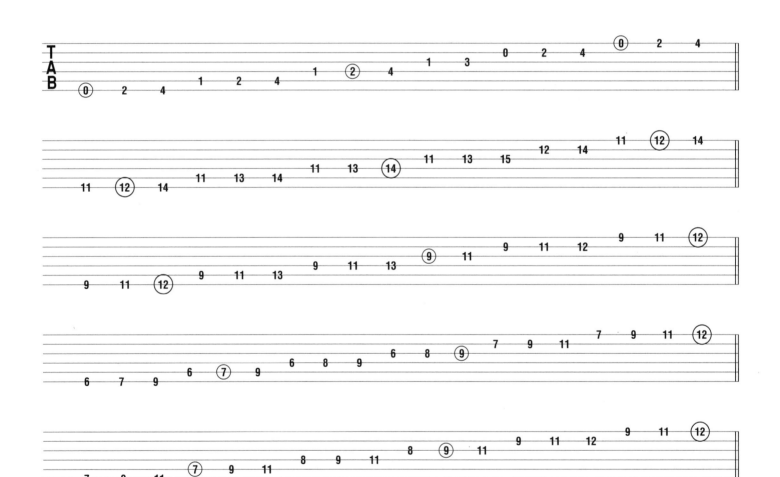

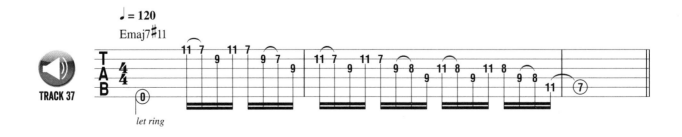

# F LYDIAN

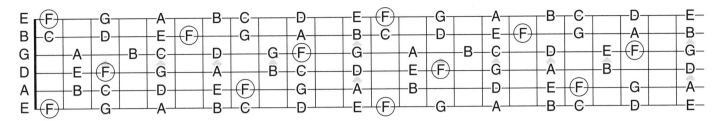

F G A B C D E          1 2 3♯4 5 6 7

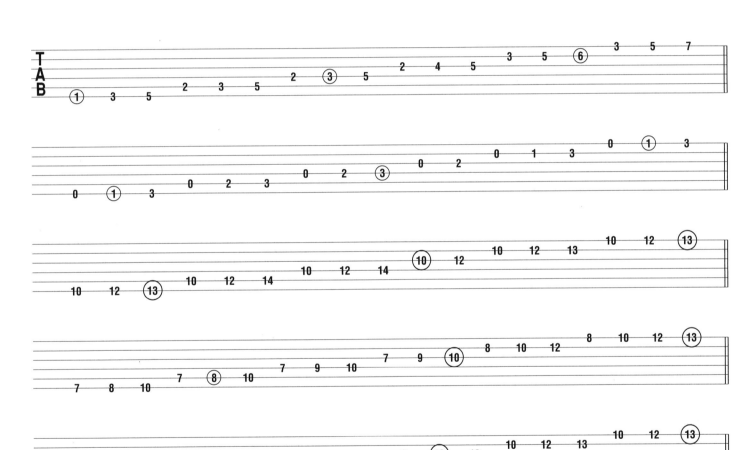

♩ = 126

Fmaj7♯11

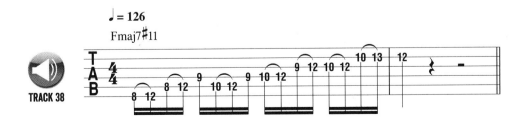

TRACK 38

# F#/Gb LYDIAN

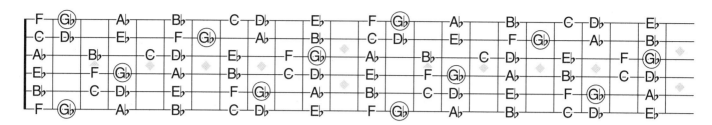

Gb Ab Bb C Db Eb F        1 2 3 #4 5 6 7

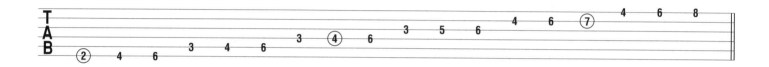

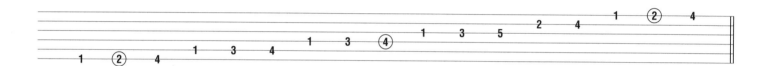

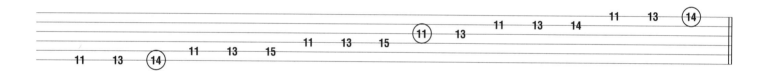

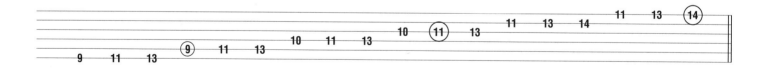

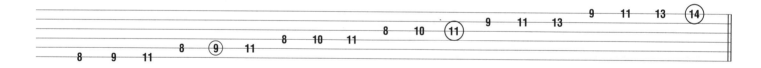

♩ = 112

Gbmaj7#11

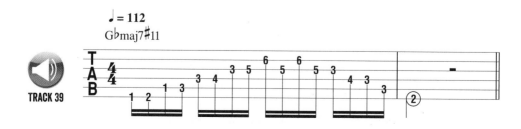

TRACK 39

# G LYDIAN

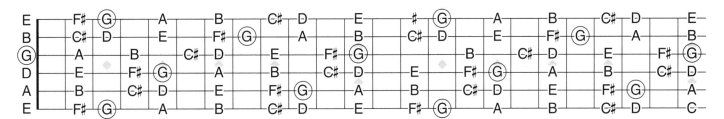

G A B C# D E F#     1 2 3 #4 5 6 7

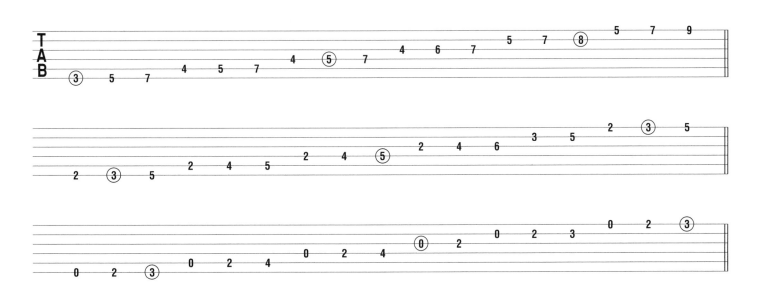

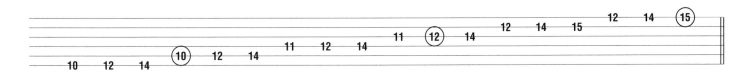

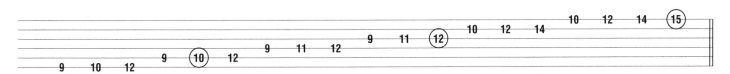

♩ = 75

**TRACK 40**  Gmaj7#11

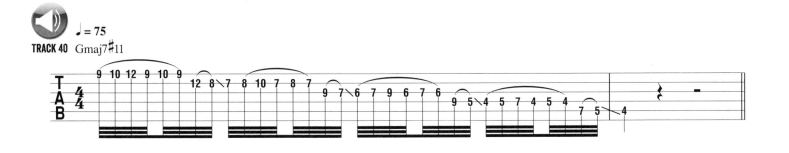

# G#/Ab LYDIAN

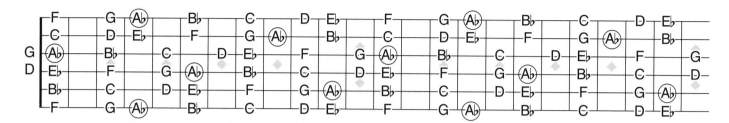

Ab Bb C D Eb F G        1 2 3 #4 5 6 7

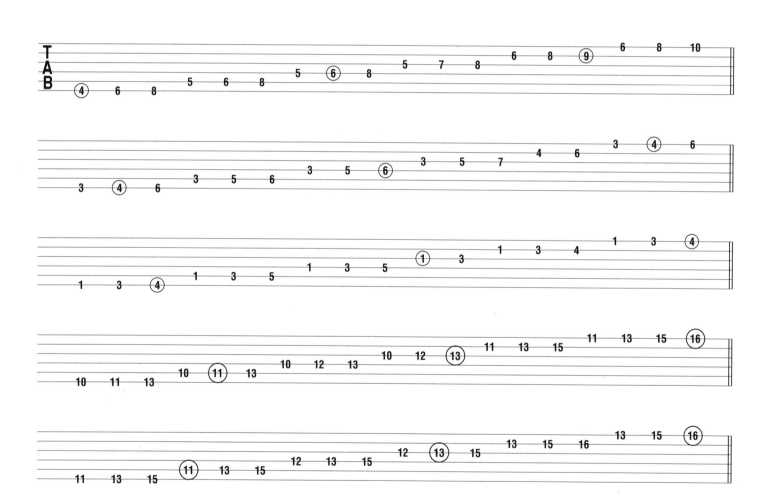

♩ = 88

Abmaj7#11

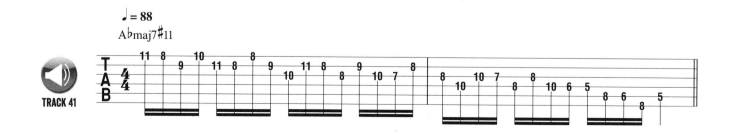

TRACK 41

# A LYDIAN

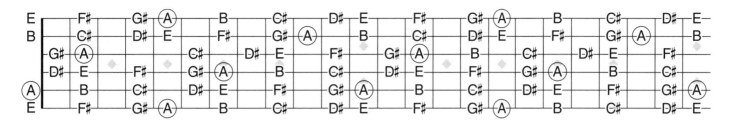

A B C# D# E F# G#        1 2 3 #4 5 6 7

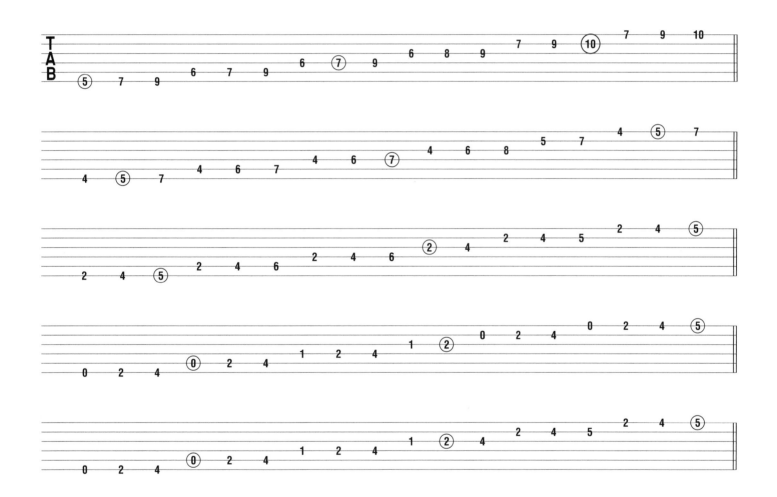

♩ = 120
Amaj7#11

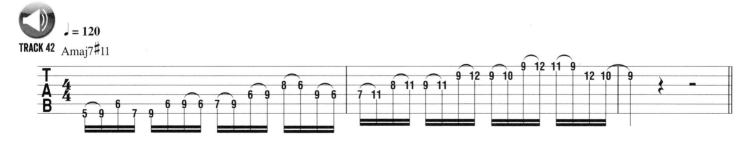

# A#/Bb LYDIAN

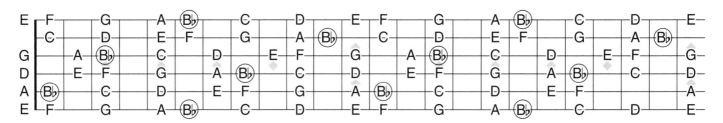

Bb C D E F G A        1 2 3 #4 5 6 7

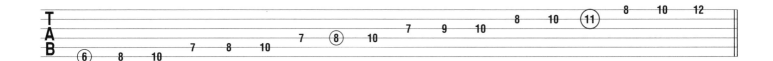

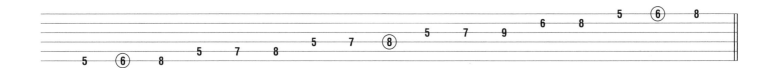

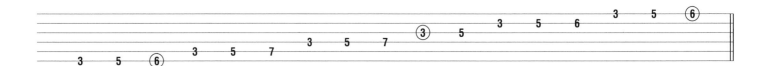

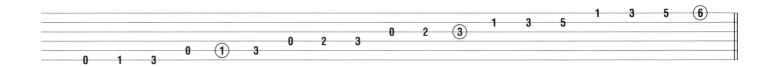

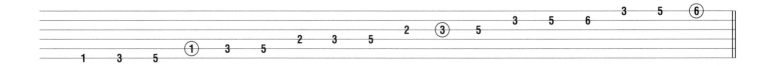

♩ = 130

Bbmaj7#11

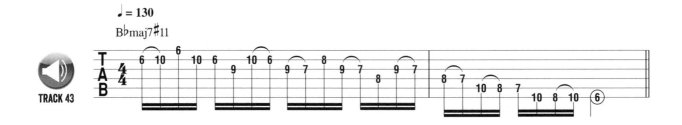

TRACK 43

# B LYDIAN

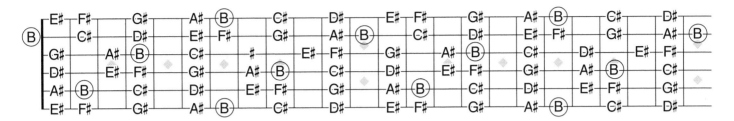

B C# D# E# F# G# A#     1 2 3 #4 5 6 7

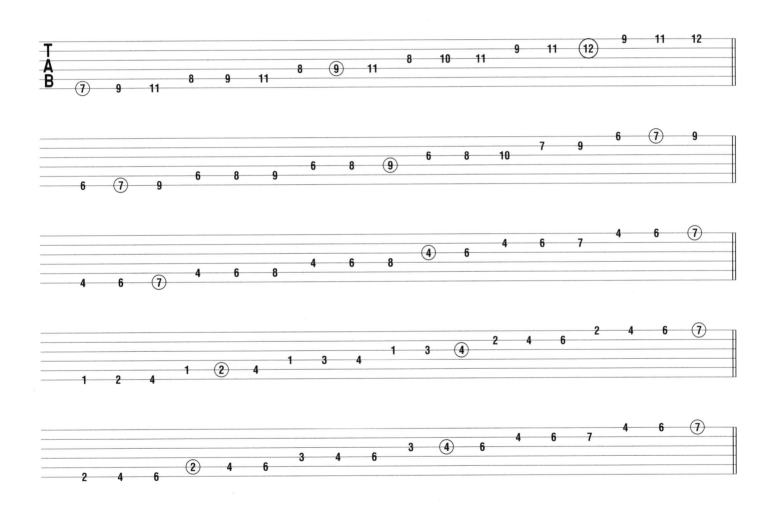

♩ = 60
Bmaj7#11

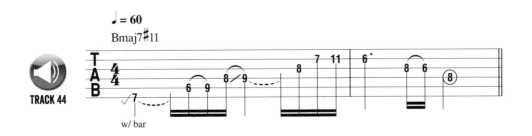

TRACK 44

w/ bar

# C LYDIAN

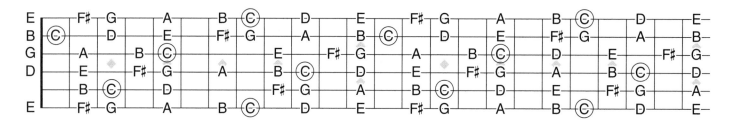

C D E F♯ G A B          1 2 3 ♯4 5 6 7

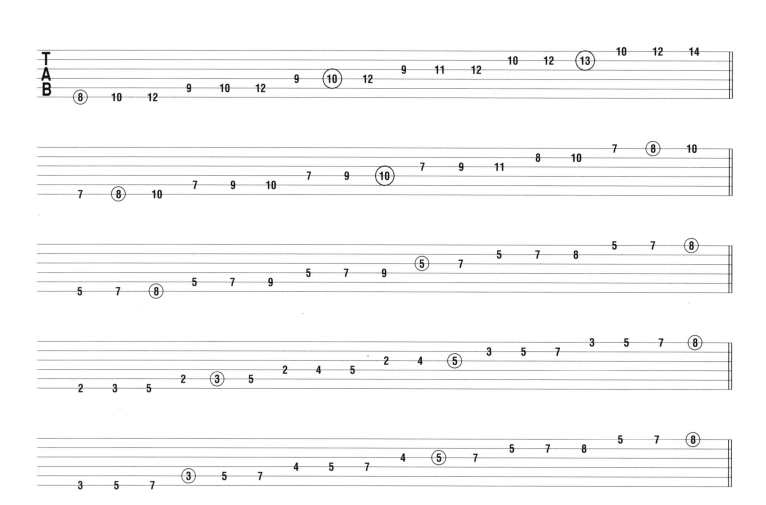

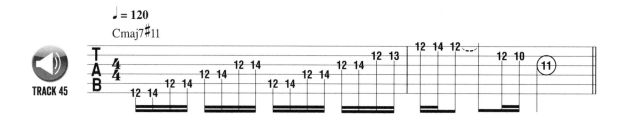

# C#/Db LYDIAN

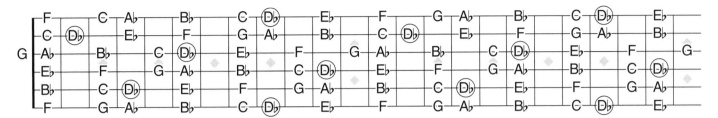

Db Eb F G Ab Bb C          1 2 3 #4 5 6 7

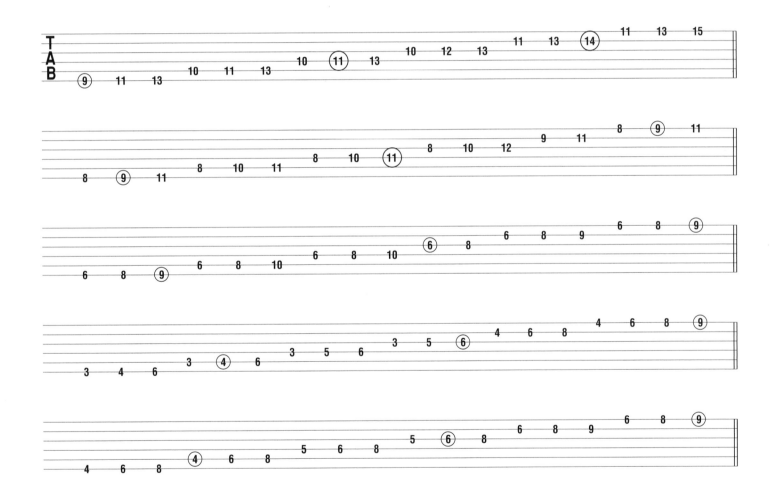

♩ = 130

Dbmaj7#11

TRACK 46

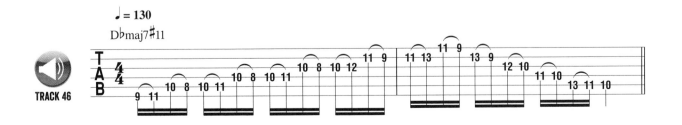

# D LYDIAN

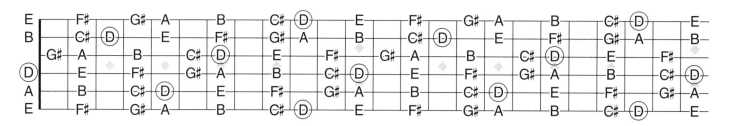

D E F♯ G♯ A B C♯          1 2 3 ♯4 5 6 7

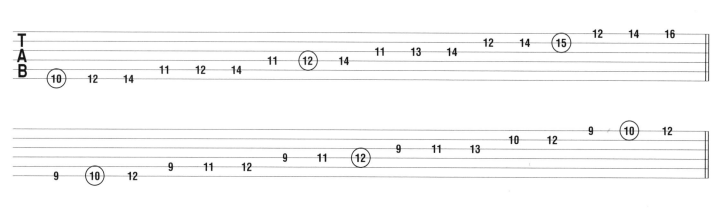

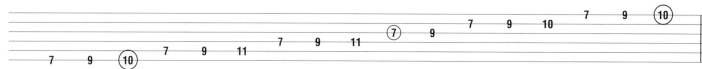

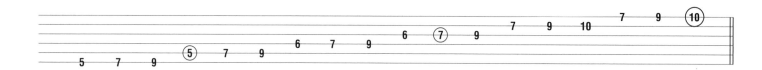

♩ = 70

**TRACK 47**  Dmaj7♯11

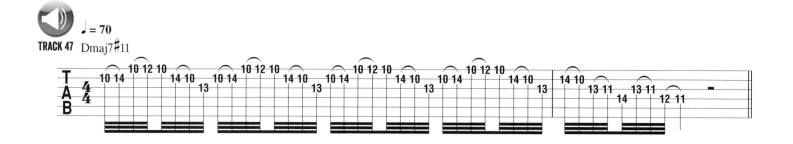

# D#/E♭ LYDIAN

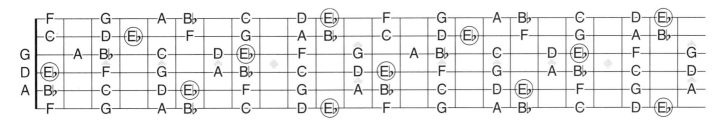

E♭ F G A B♭ C D      1 2 3 #4 5 6 7

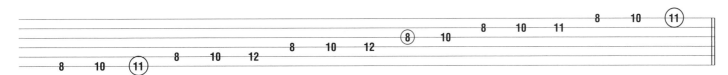

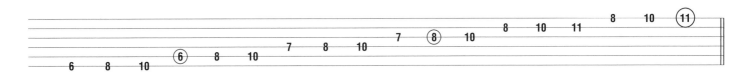

♩ = 176

**TRACK 48**  E♭maj7#11

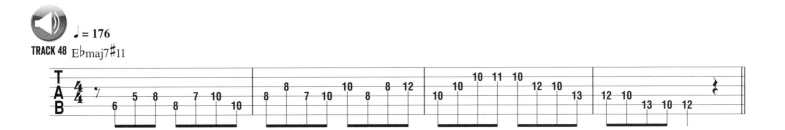

# E MIXOLYDIAN

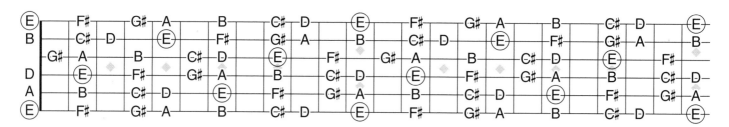

E F♯ G♯ A B C♯ D      1 2 3 4 5 6 ♭7

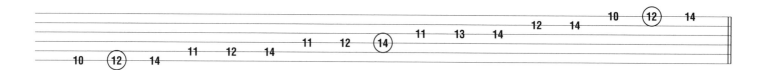

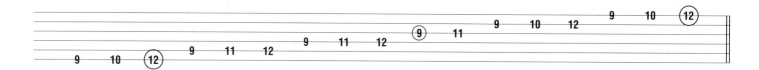

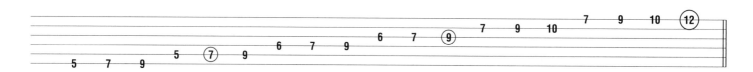

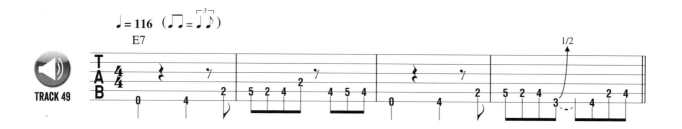

# F MIXOLYDIAN

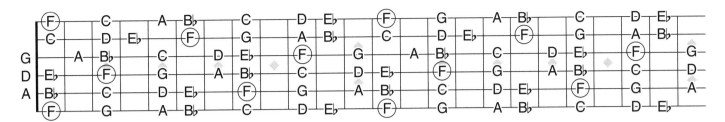

F G A Bb C D Eb

1 2 3 4 5 6 b7

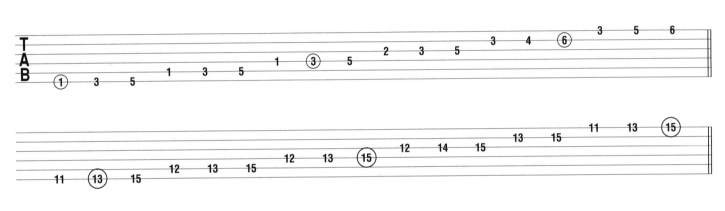

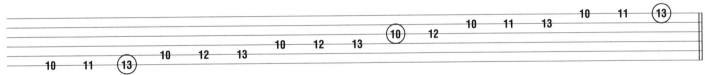

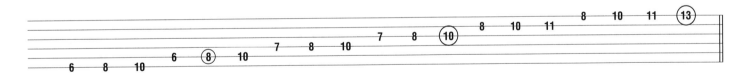

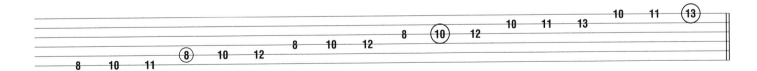

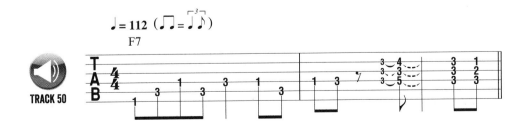

TRACK 50

# F#/Gb MIXOLYDIAN

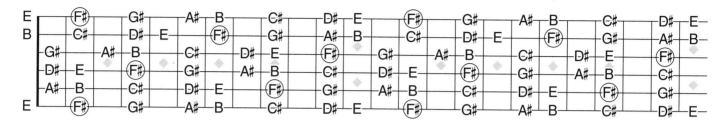

F# G# A# B C# D# E        1 2 3 4 5 6 ♭7

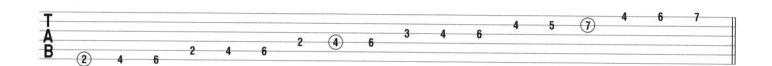

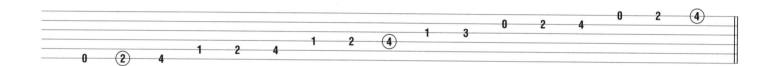

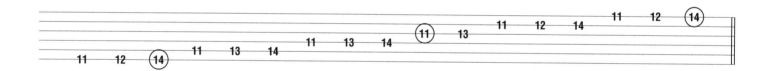

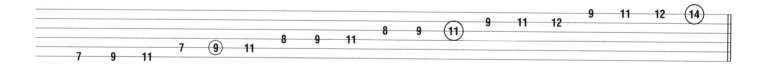

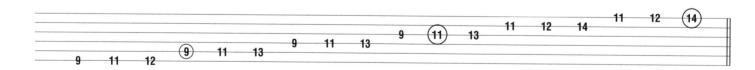

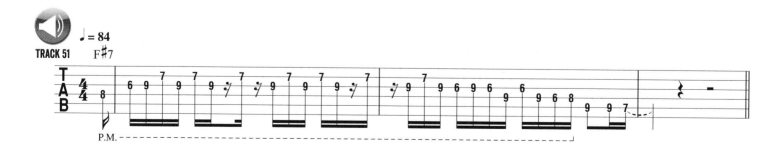

TRACK 51        ♩ = 84        F#7

P.M.

64

# G MIXOLYDIAN

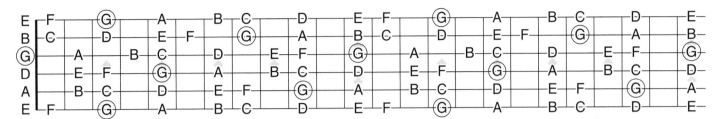

G A B C D E F          1 2 3 4 5 6 ♭7

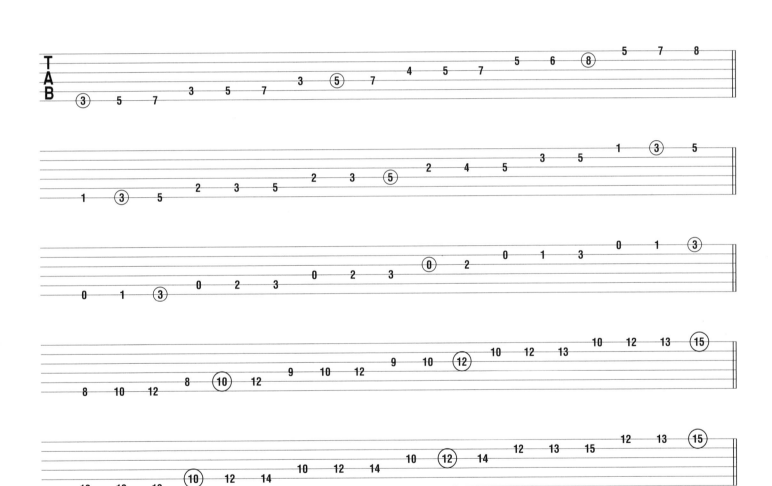

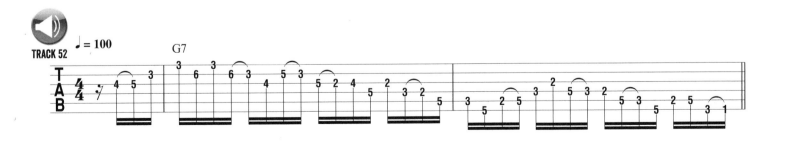

TRACK 52   ♩ = 100

# G#/Ab MIXOLYDIAN

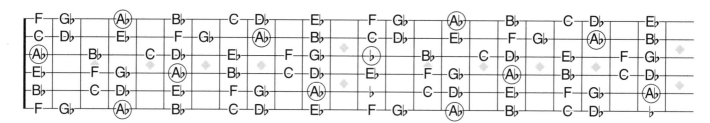

Ab Bb C Db Eb F Gb          1 2 3 4 5 6 b7

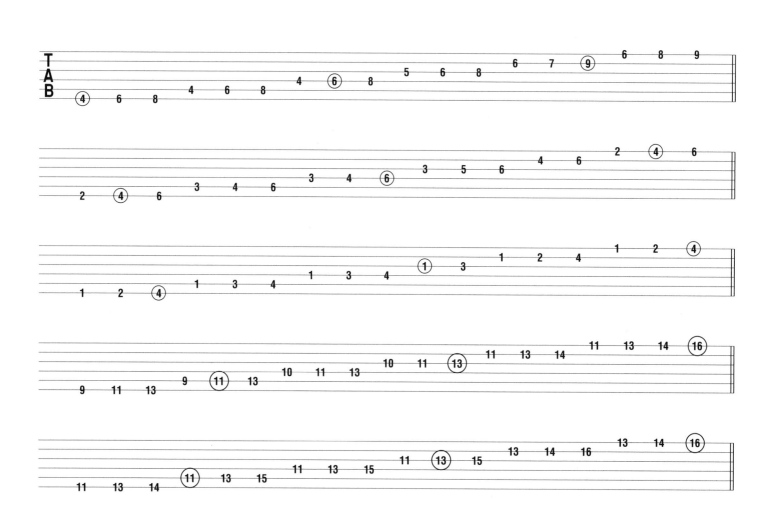

♩ = 120

TRACK 53    Ab13sus4

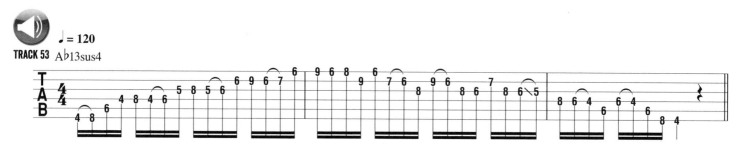

# A MIXOLYDIAN

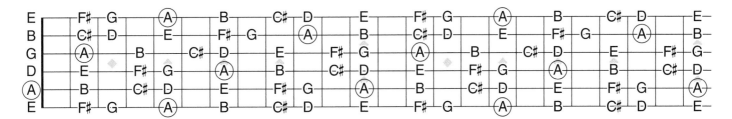

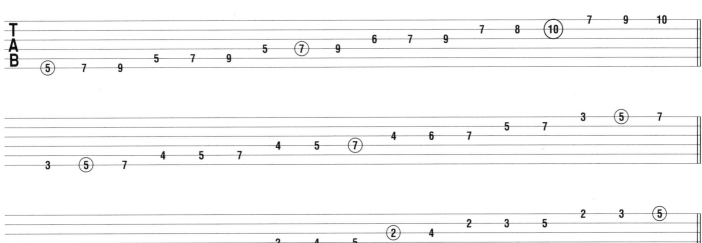

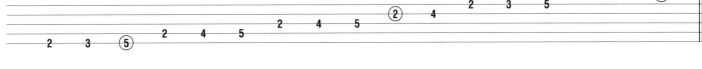

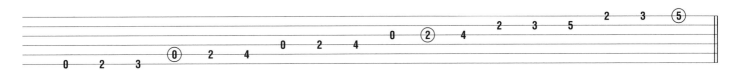

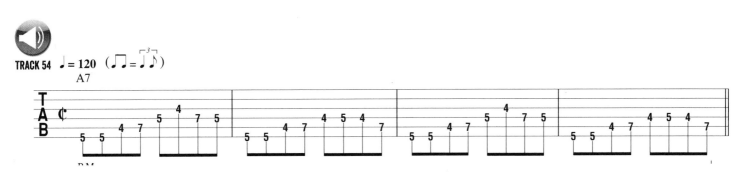

# A#/Bb MIXOLYDIAN

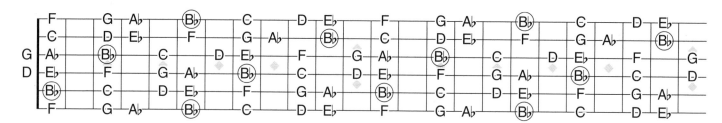

Bb C D Eb F G Ab          1 2 3 4 5 6 b7

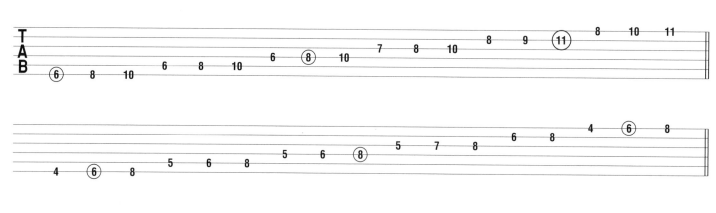

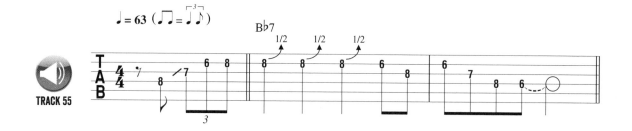

# B MIXOLYDIAN

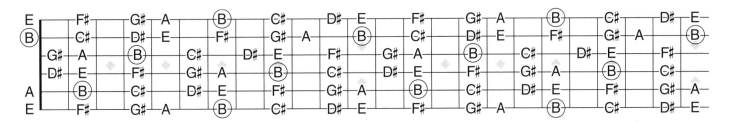

B C# D# E F# G# A          1 2 3 4 5 6 b7

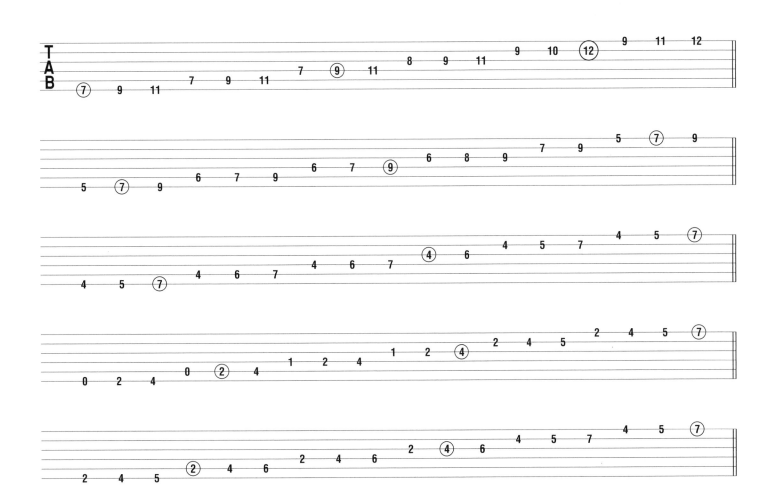

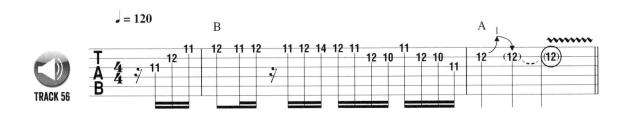

# C MIXOLYDIAN

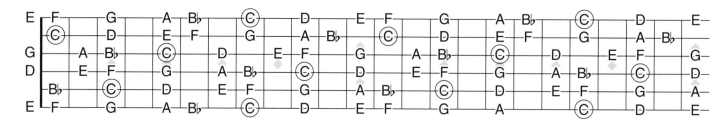

C D E F G A B♭        1 2 3 4 5 6 ♭7

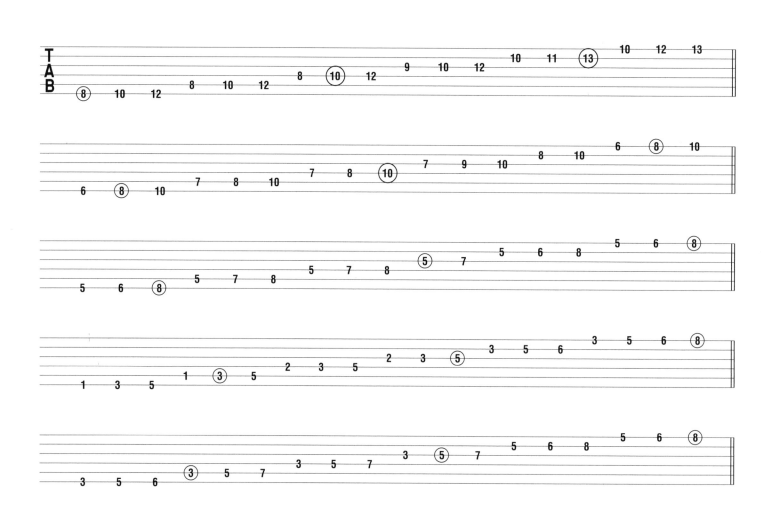

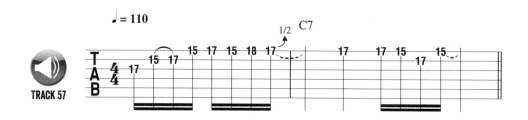

TRACK 57

# C♯/D♭ MIXOLYDIAN

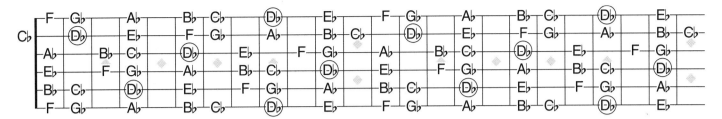

D♭ E♭ F G♭ A♭ B♭ C♭          1 2 3 4 5 6 ♭7

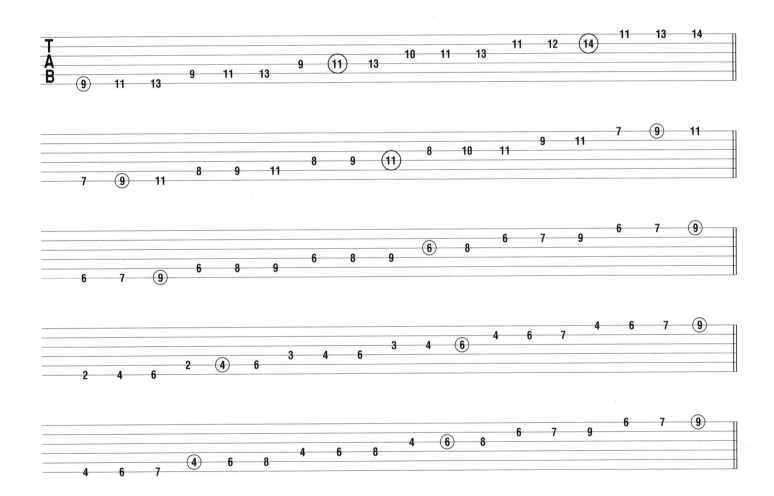

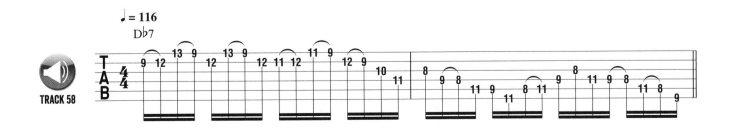

# D MIXOLYDIAN

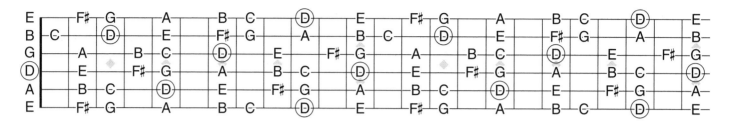

D E F# G A B C          1 2 3 4 5 6 ♭7

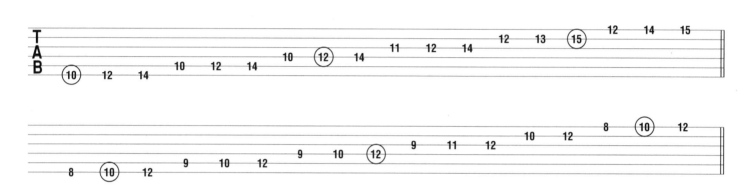

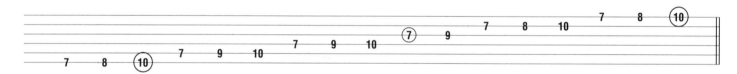

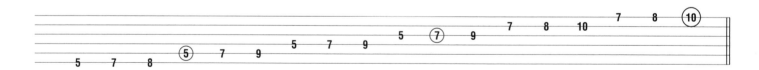

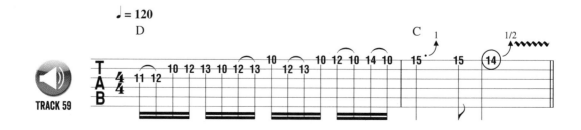

TRACK 59

# D#/E♭ MIXOLYDIAN

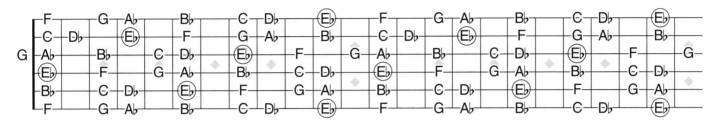

E♭ F G A♭ B♭ C D♭      1 2 3 4 5 6 ♭7

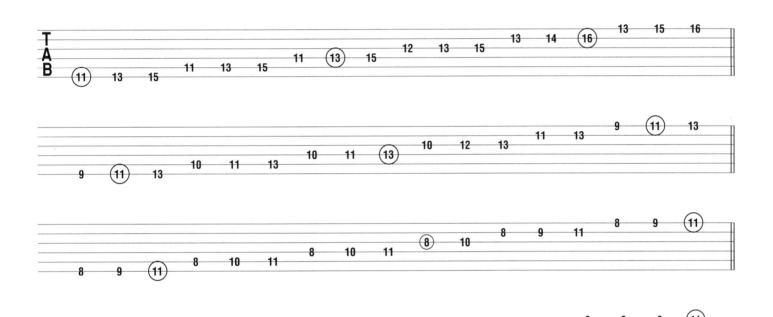

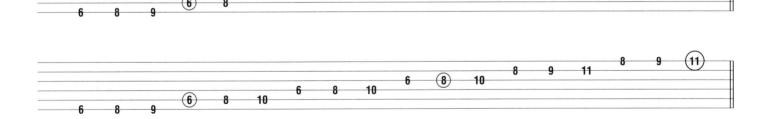

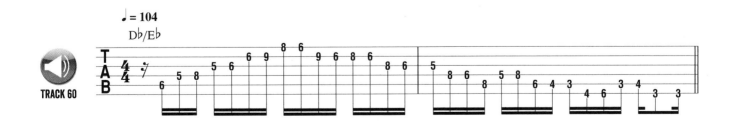

# E NATURAL MINOR (AEOLIAN)

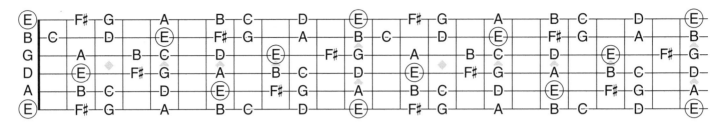

E F# G A B C D          1 2 ♭3 4 5 ♭6 ♭7

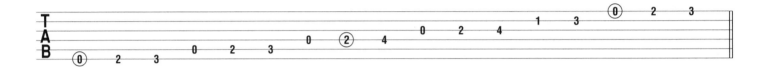

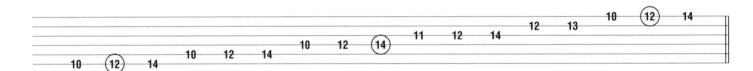

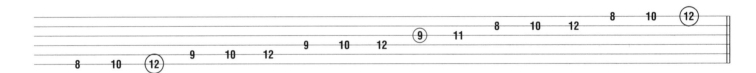

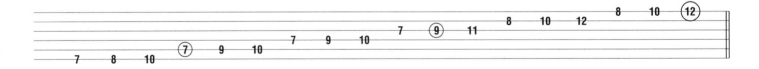

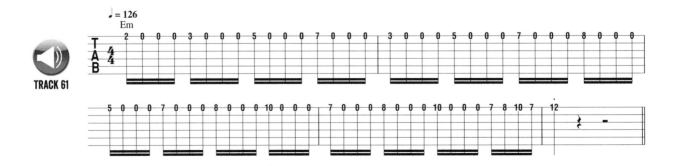

74

# F NATURAL MINOR (AEOLIAN)

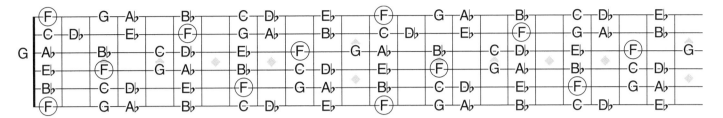

F G Ab Bb C Db Eb        1 2 b3 4 5 b6 b7

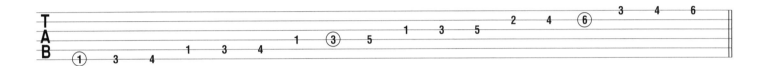

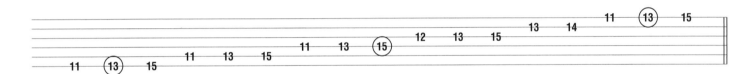

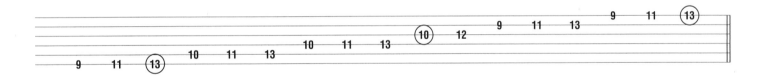

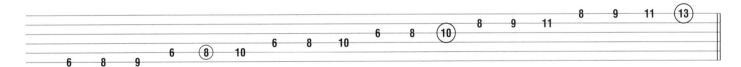

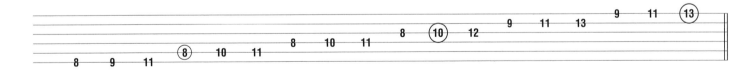

♩ = 130

TRACK 62

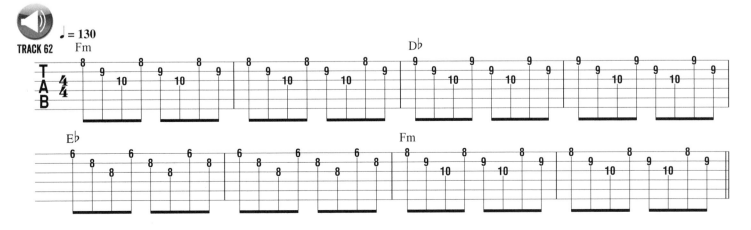

# F#/Gb NATURAL MINOR (AEOLIAN)

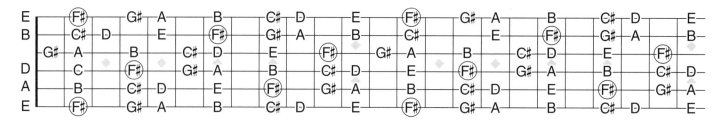

F# G# A B C# D E        1 2 b3 4 5 b6 b7

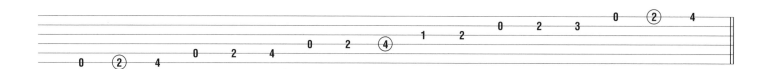

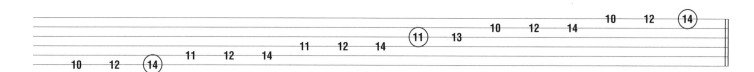

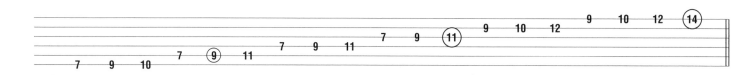

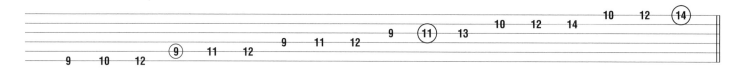

**TRACK 63**  ♩ = 144

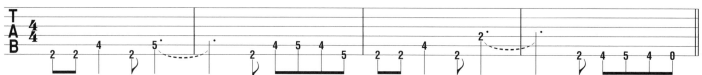

# G NATURAL MINOR (AEOLIAN)

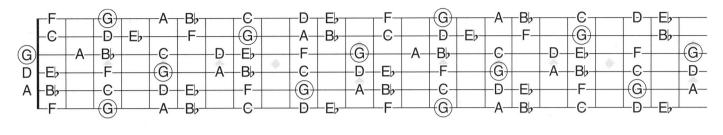

G A B♭ C D E♭ F        1 2 ♭3 4 5 ♭6 ♭7

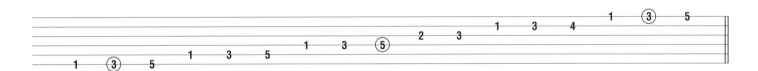

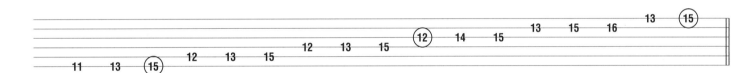

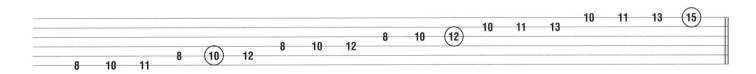

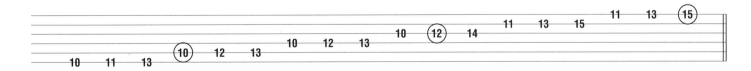

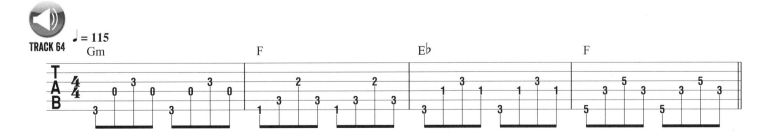

TRACK 64  ♩ = 115

# G#/Ab NATURAL MINOR (AEOLIAN)

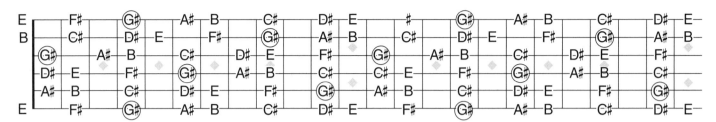

G# A# B C# D# E F#          1 2 b3 4 5 b6 b7

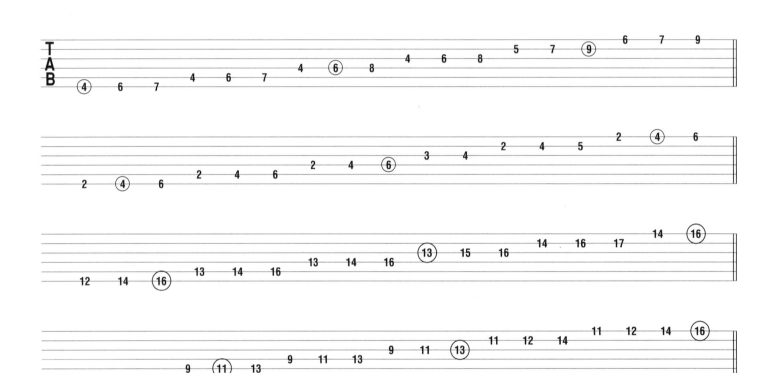

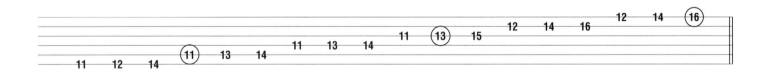

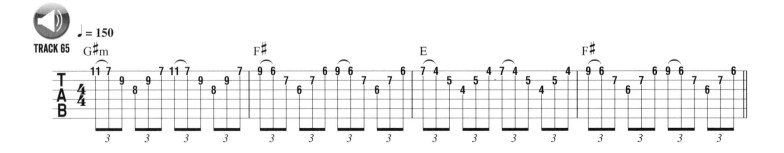

# A NATURAL MINOR (AEOLIAN)

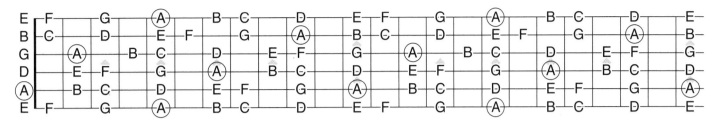

A B C D E F G          1 2 ♭3 4 5 ♭6 ♭7

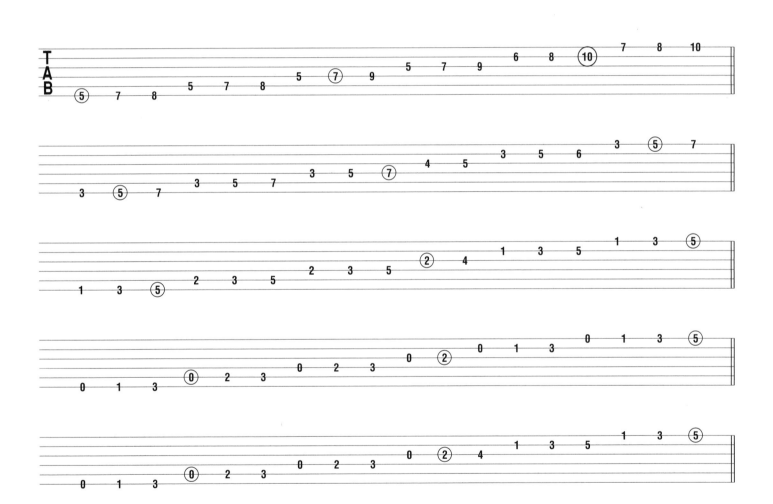

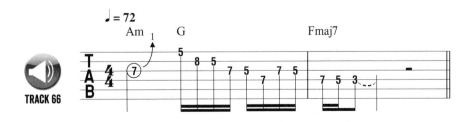

TRACK 66

# A#/Bb NATURAL MINOR (AEOLIAN)

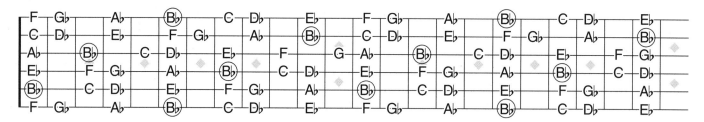

Bb C Db Eb F Gb Ab        1 2 b3 4 5 b6 b7

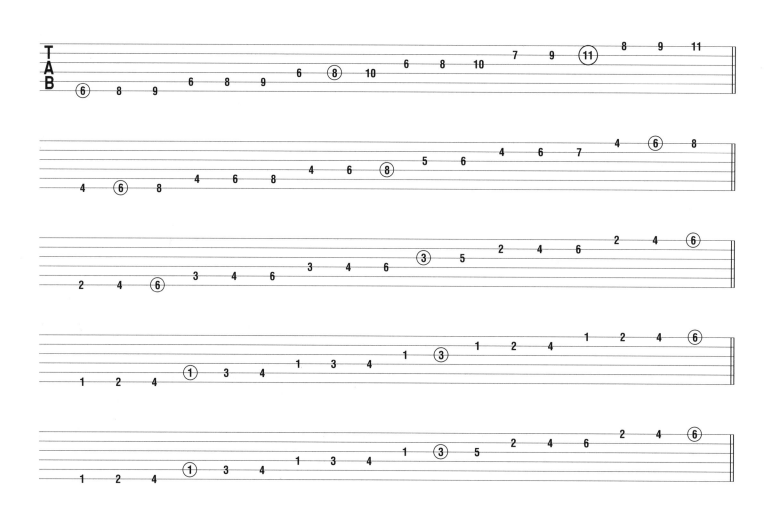

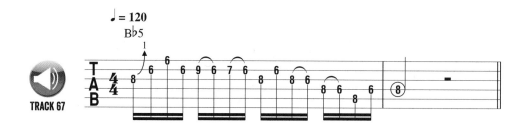

# B NATURAL MINOR (AEOLIAN)

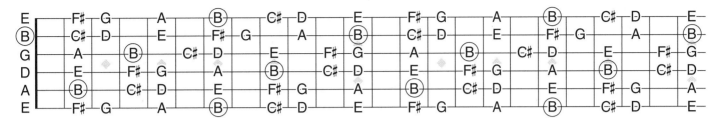

B C# D E F# G A          1 2 b3 4 5 b6 b7

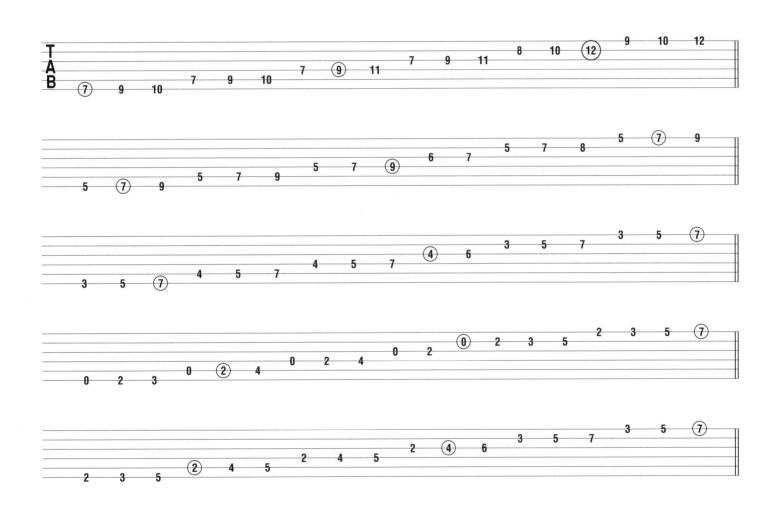

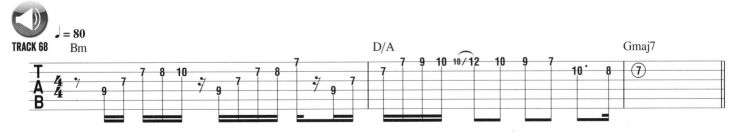

TRACK 68

♩ = 80

# C NATURAL MINOR (AEOLIAN)

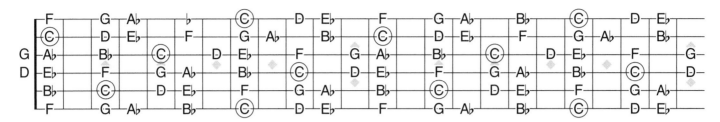

C D E♭ F G A♭ B♭          1 2 ♭3 4 5 ♭6 ♭7

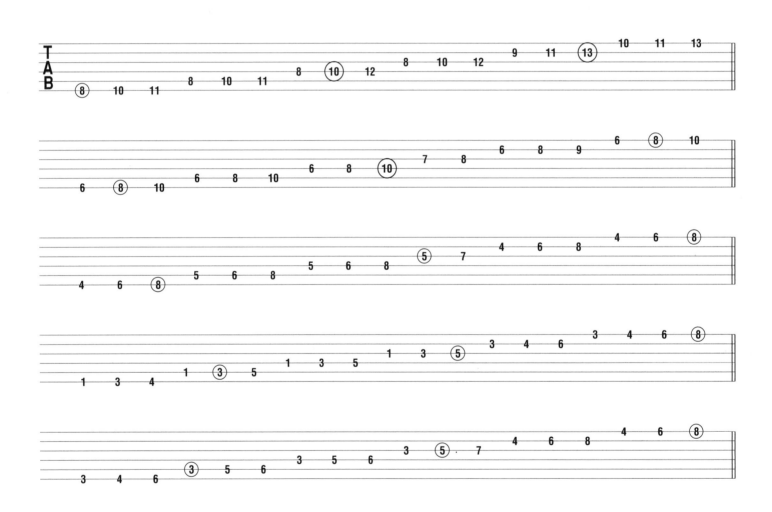

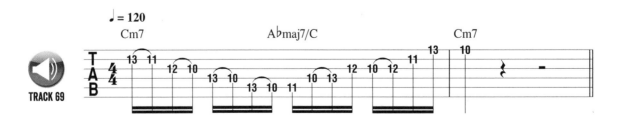

# C#/Db NATURAL MINOR (AEOLIAN)

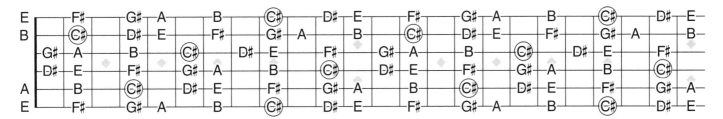

C# D# E F# G# A B        1 2 b3 4 5 b6 b7

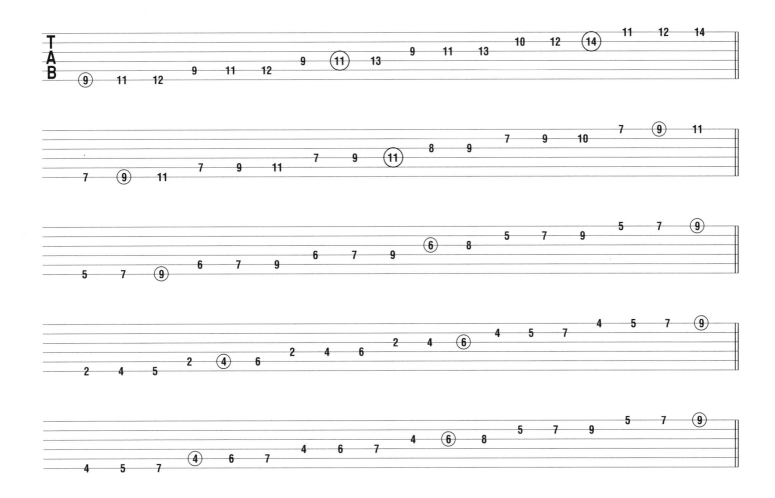

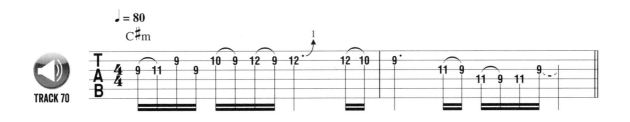

# D NATURAL MINOR (AEOLIAN)

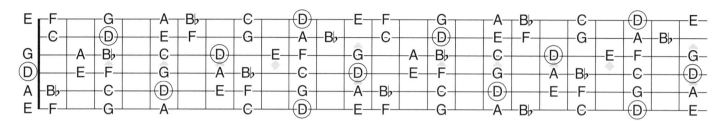

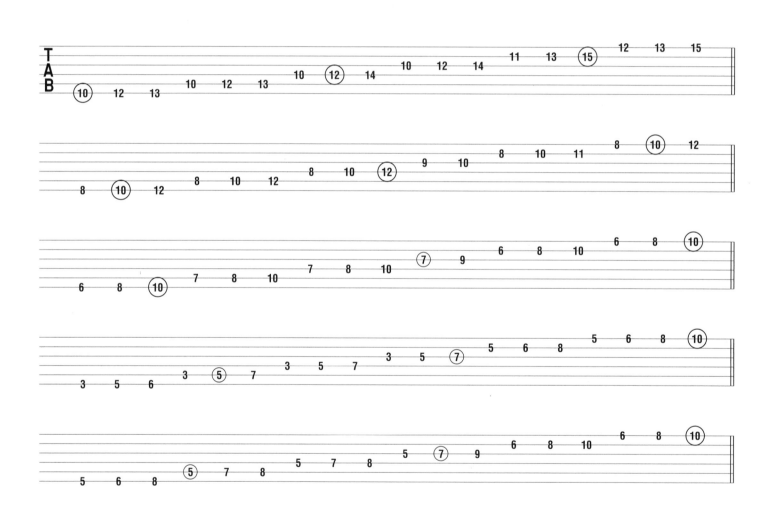

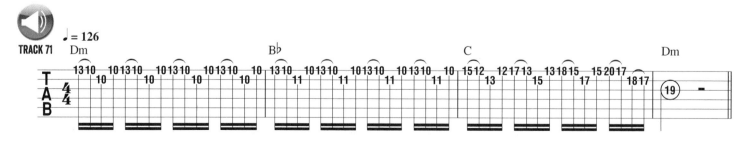

# D#/E♭ NATURAL MINOR (AEOLIAN)

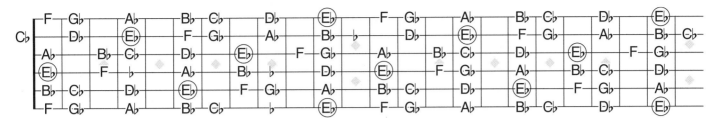

E♭ F G♭ A♭ B♭ C♭ D♭        1 2 ♭3 4 5 ♭6 ♭7

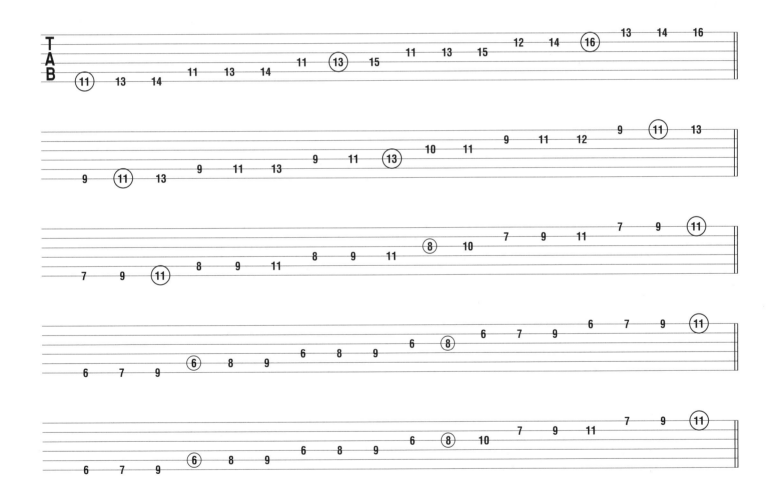

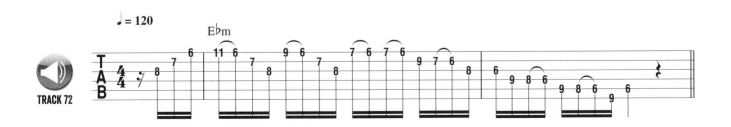

# E LOCRIAN

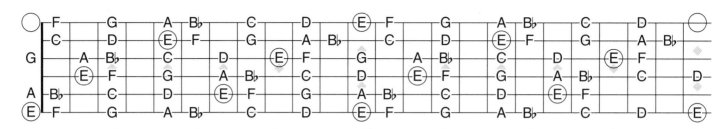

E F G A B♭ C D        1 ♭2 ♭3 4 ♭5 ♭6 ♭7

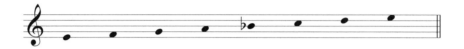

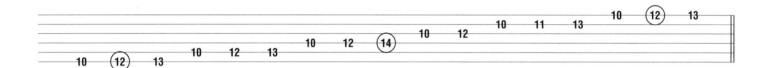

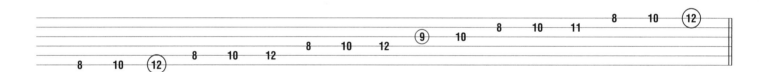

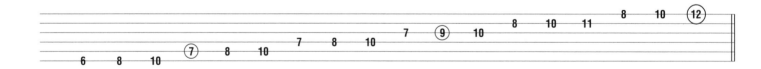

**TRACK 73**   ♩ = 126
Em7♭5

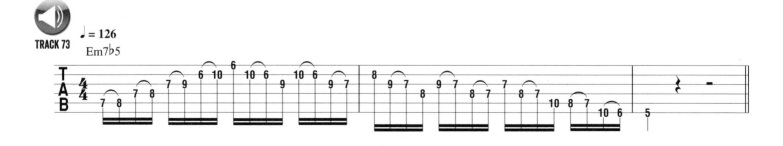

# F LOCRIAN

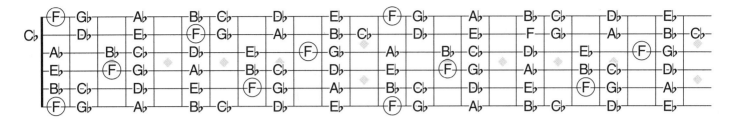

F Gb Ab Bb Cb Db Eb          1 b2 b3 4 b5 b6 b7

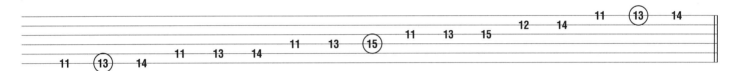

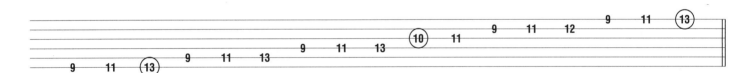

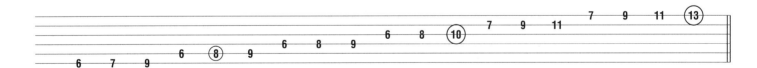

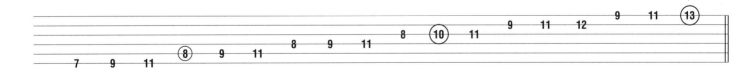

**TRACK 74**  ♩ = 126  Fm7b5

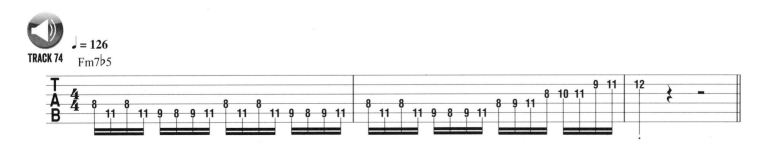

# F#/Gb LOCRIAN

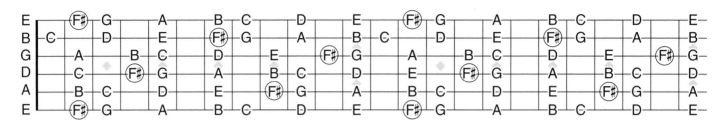

F# G A B C D E          1 ♭2 ♭3 4 ♭5 ♭6 ♭7

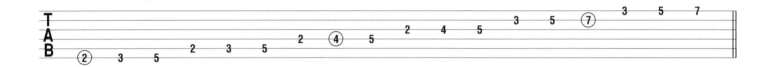

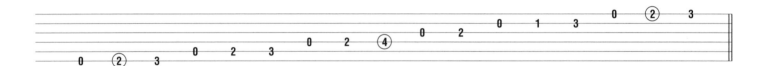

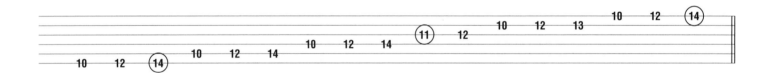

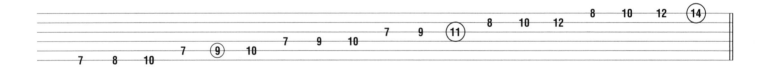

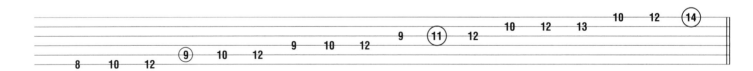

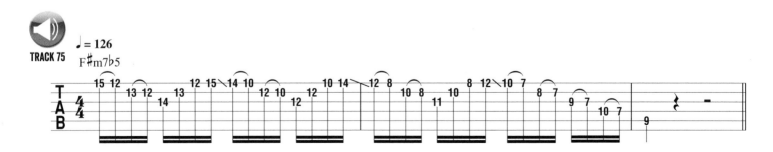

♩ = 126

TRACK 75

F#m7♭5

# G LOCRIAN

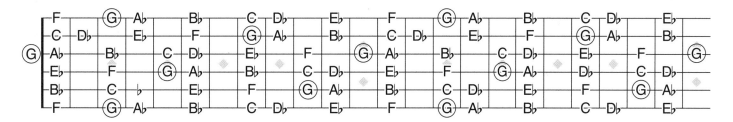

G A♭ B♭ C D♭ E♭ F          1 ♭2 ♭3 4 ♭5 ♭6 ♭7

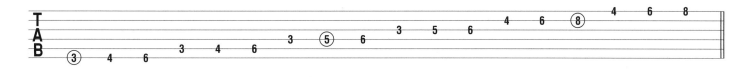

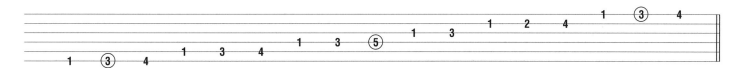

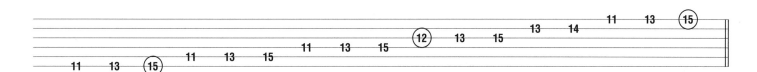

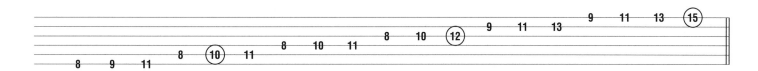

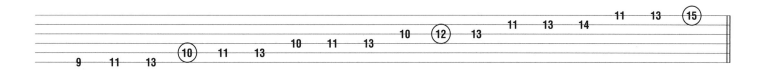

♩ = 120

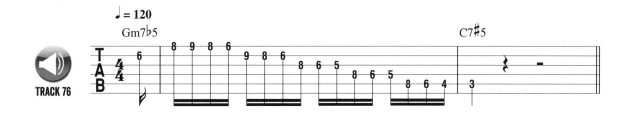

TRACK 76

# G#/Ab LOCRIAN

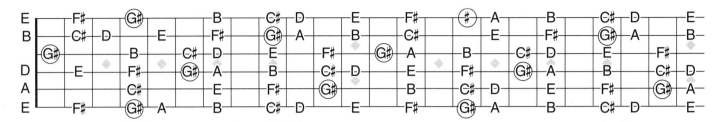

G# A B C# D E F#        1 ♭2 ♭3 4 ♭5 ♭6 ♭7

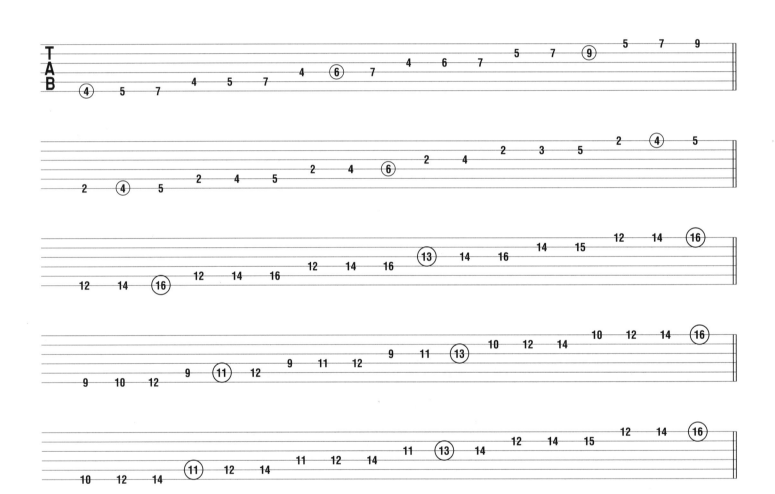

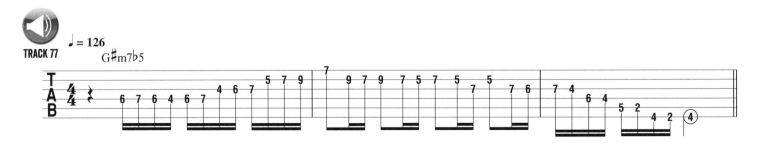

TRACK 77

♩ = 126

G#m7♭5

# A LOCRIAN

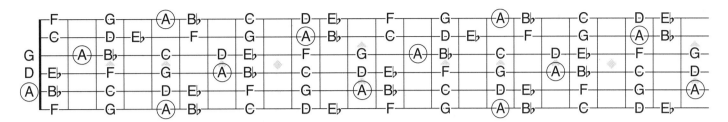

A Bb C D Eb F G          1 b2 b3 4 b5 b6 b7

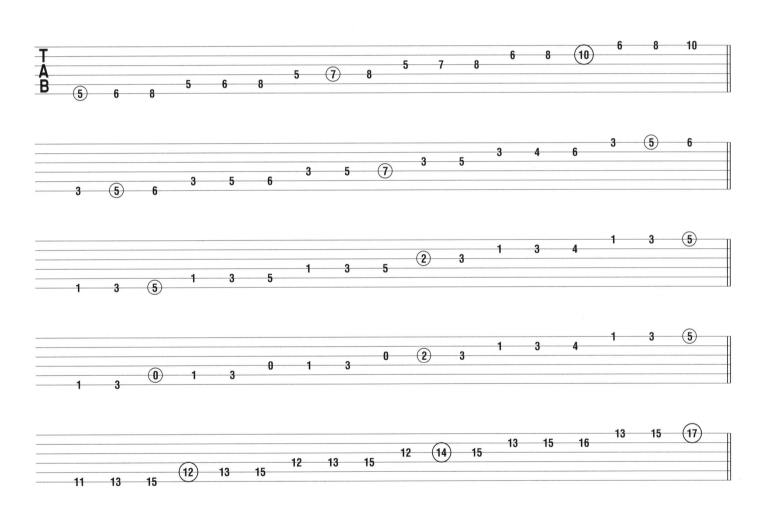

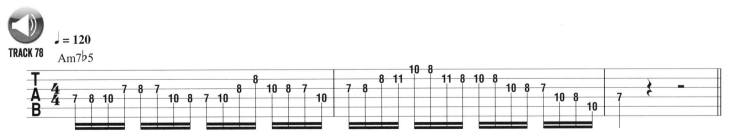

**TRACK 78**

♩ = 120

Am7b5

# A#/B♭ LOCRIAN

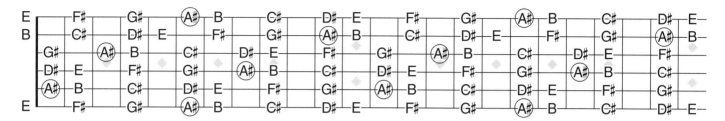

A# B C# D# E F# G#    1 ♭2 ♭3 4 ♭5 ♭6 ♭7

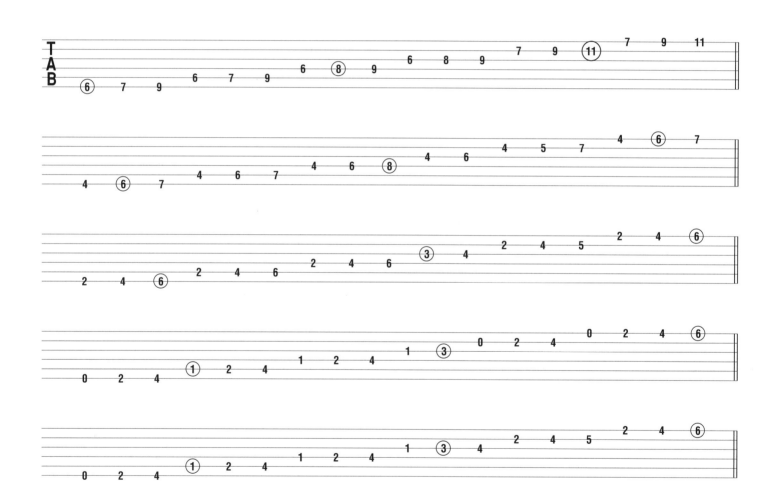

**TRACK 79**    ♩ = 160

A#m7♭5

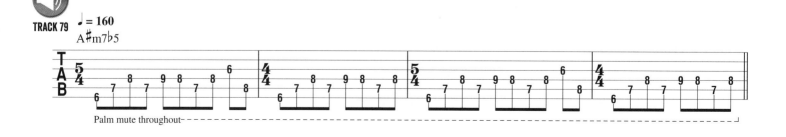

Palm mute throughout

# B LOCRIAN

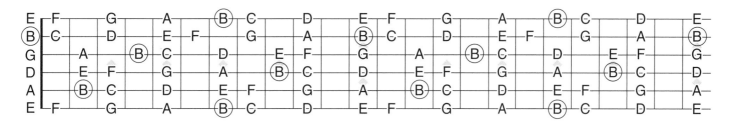

B C D E F G A       1 ♭2 ♭3 4 ♭5 ♭6 ♭7

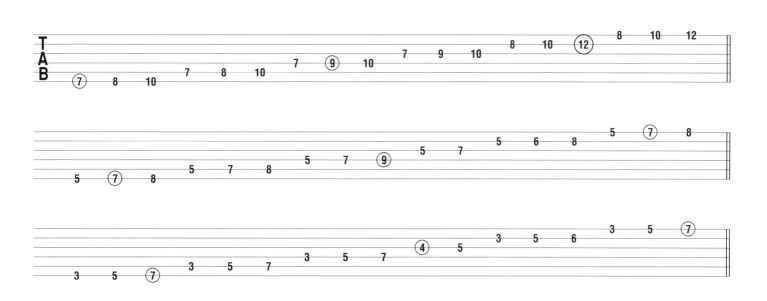

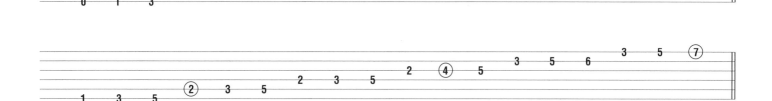

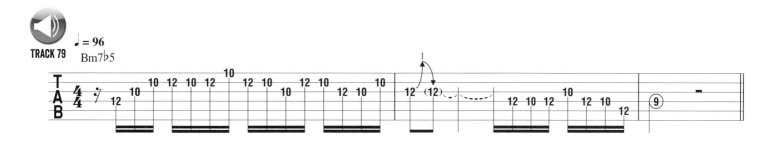

**TRACK 79**  ♩ = 96
Bm7♭5

# C LOCRIAN

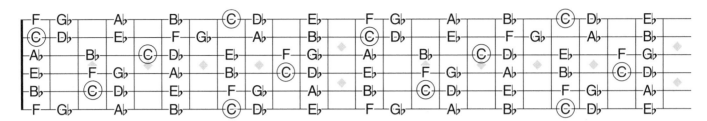

C D♭ E♭ F G♭ A♭ B♭          1 ♭2 ♭3 4 ♭5 ♭6 ♭7

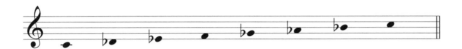

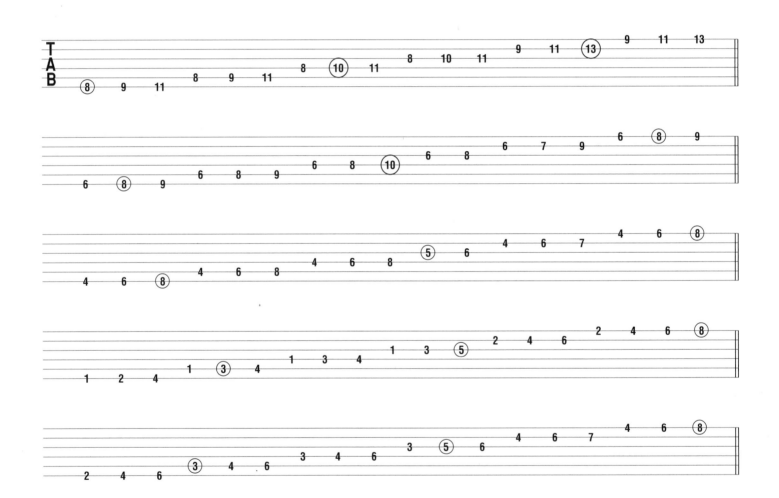

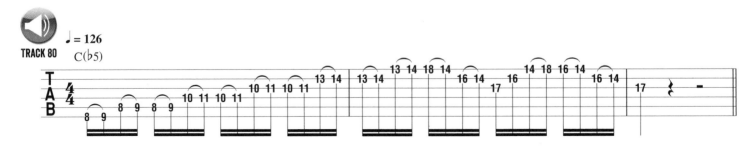

TRACK 80     ♩ = 126

C(♭5)

# C#/D♭ LOCRIAN

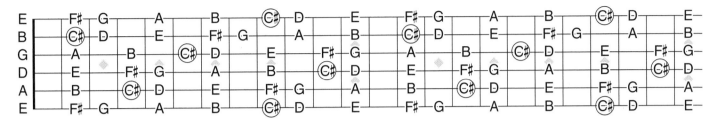

C♯ D E F♯ G A B          1 ♭2 ♭3 4 ♭5 ♭6 ♭7

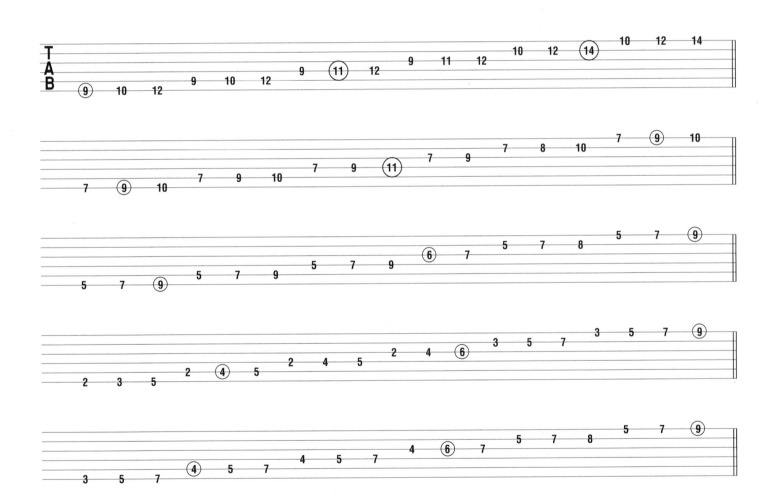

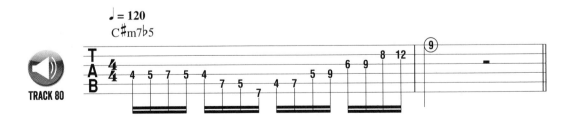

# D LOCRIAN

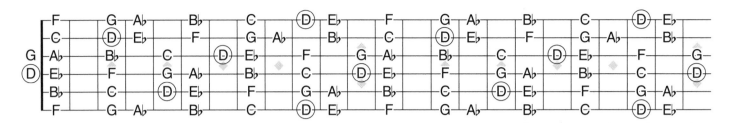

D Eb F G Ab Bb C        1 b2 b3 4 b5 b6 b7

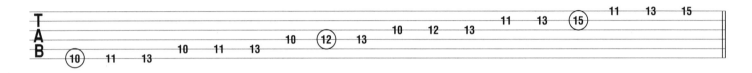

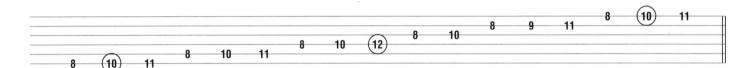

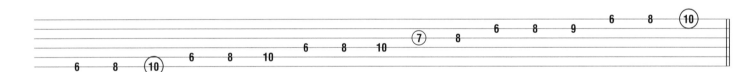

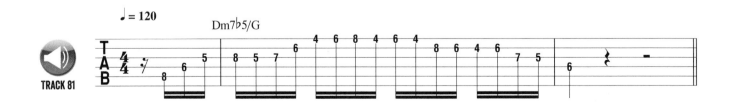

# D#/E♭ LOCRIAN

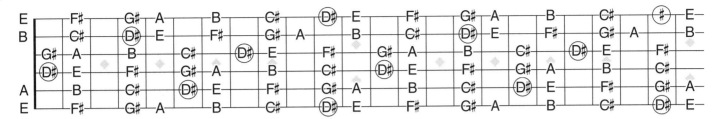

D# E F# G# A B C#          1 ♭2 ♭3 4 ♭5 ♭6 ♭7

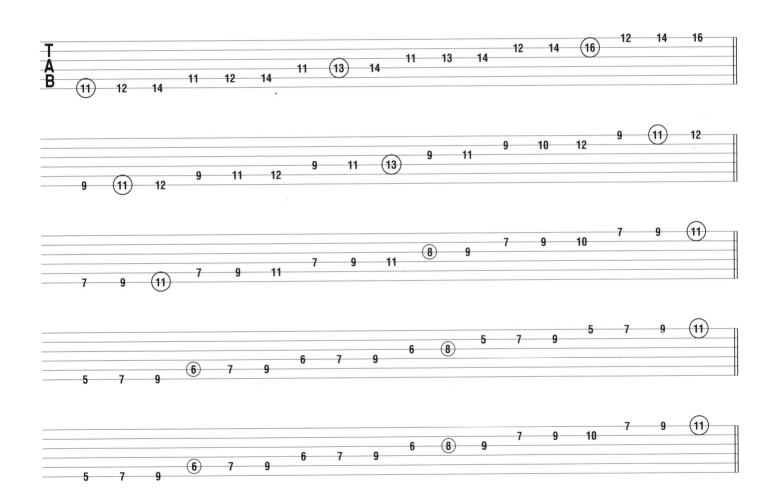

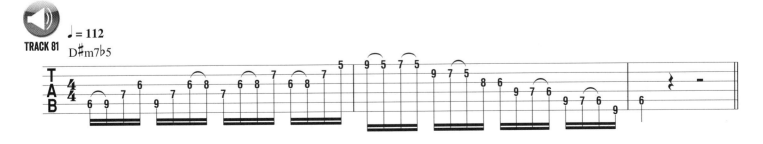

TRACK 81

♩ = 112

D#m7♭5

# E MINOR PENTATONIC

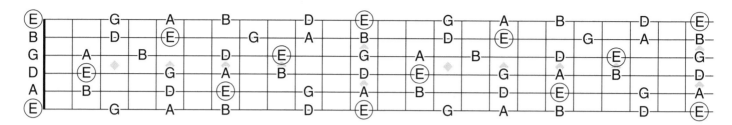

E G A B D          1 ♭3 4 5 ♭7

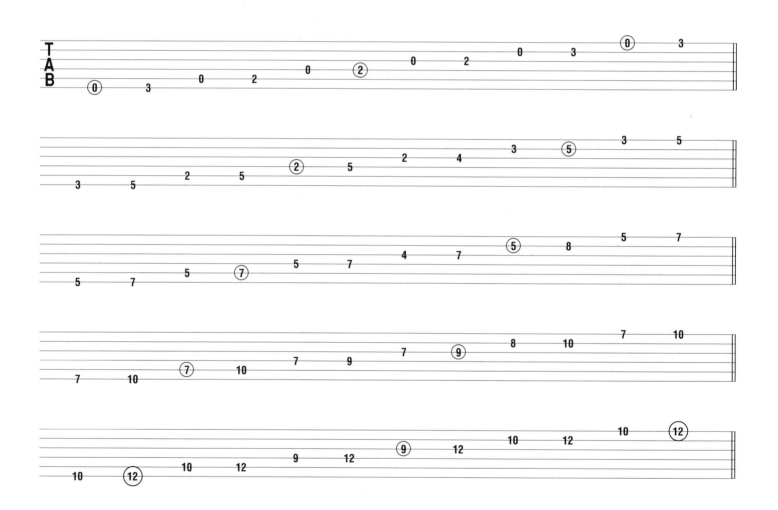

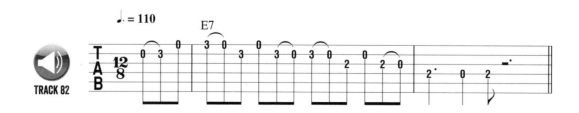

# F MINOR PENTATONIC

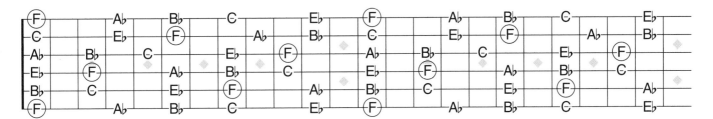

F A♭ B♭ C E♭        1 ♭3 4 5 ♭7

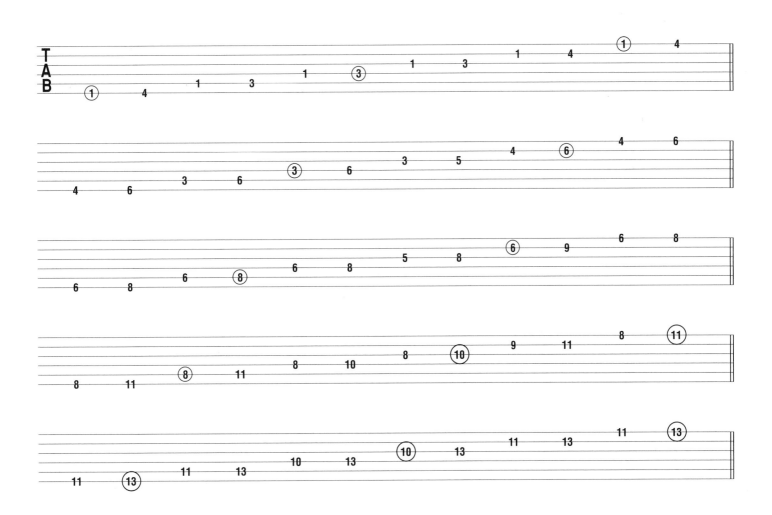

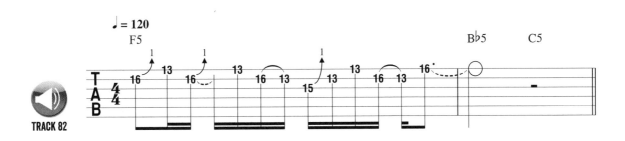

# F#/G♭ MINOR PENTATONIC

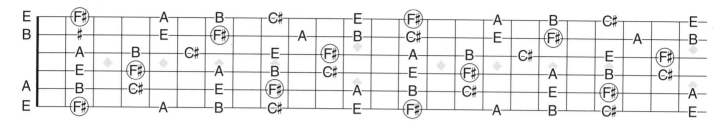

F# A B C# E          1 ♭3 4 5 ♭7

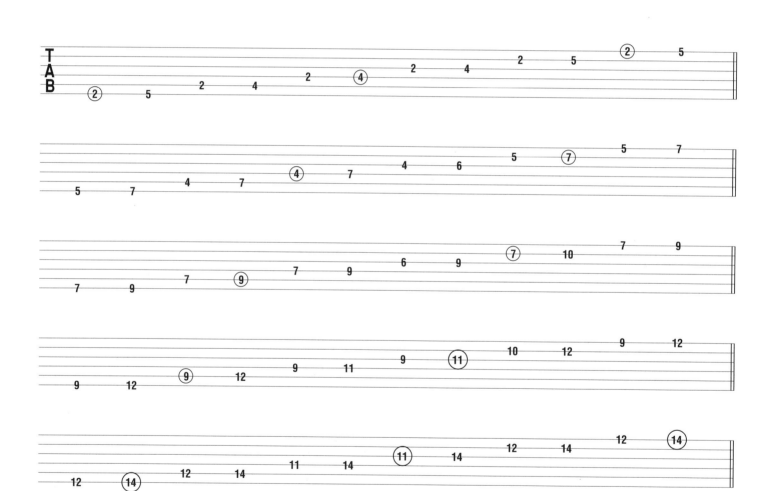

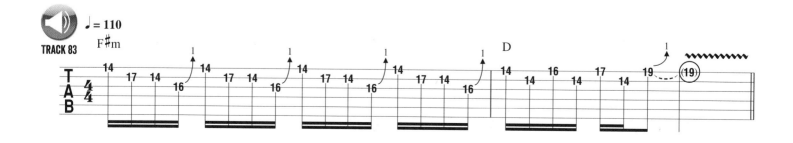

# G MINOR PENTATONIC

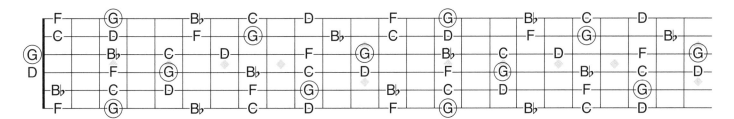

G B♭ C D F        1 ♭3 4 5 ♭7

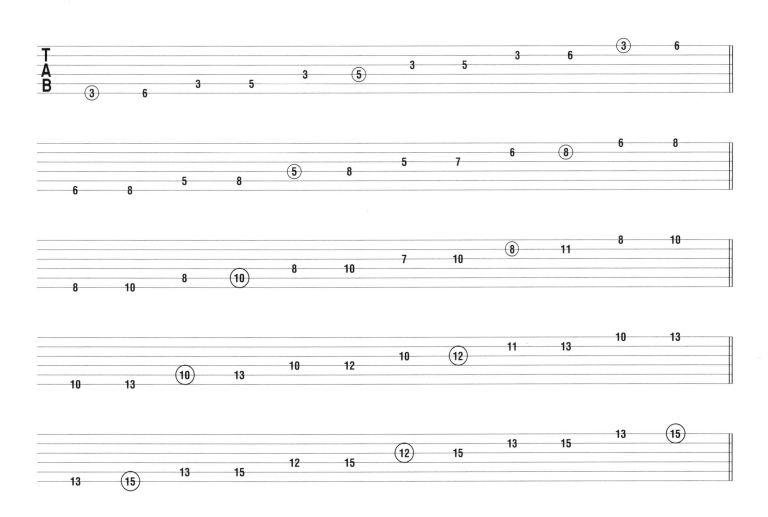

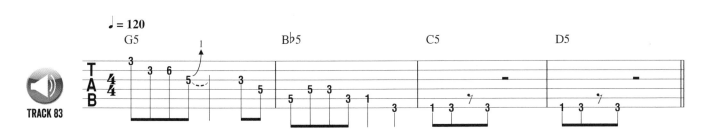

TRACK 83

# G#/Ab MINOR PENTATONIC

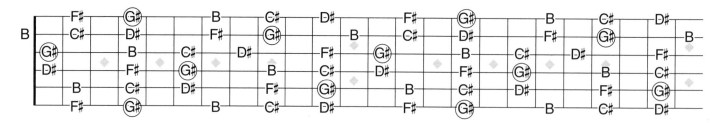

G# B C# D# F#     1 b3 4 5 b7

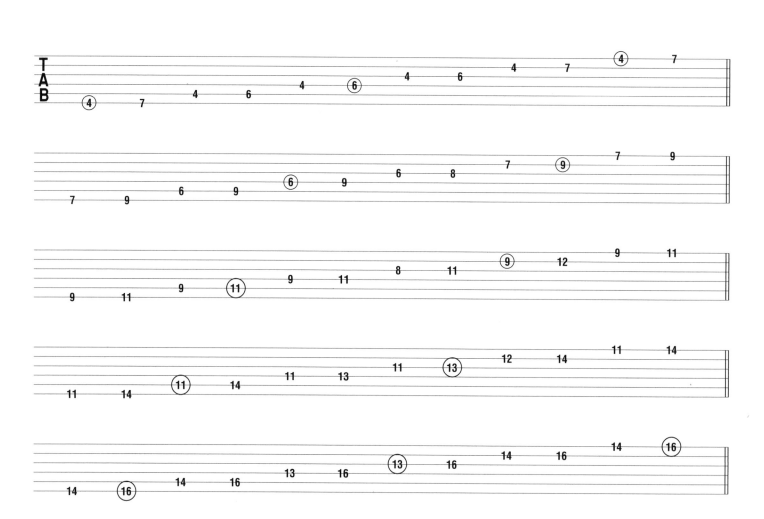

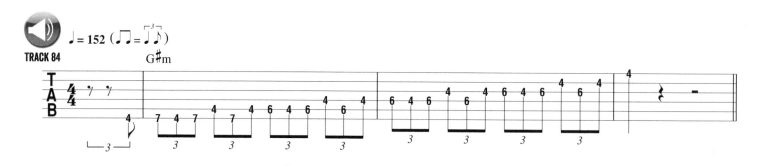

# A MINOR PENTATONIC

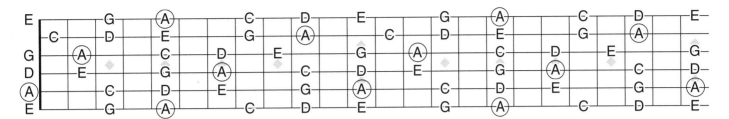

A C D E G      1 ♭3 4 5 ♭7

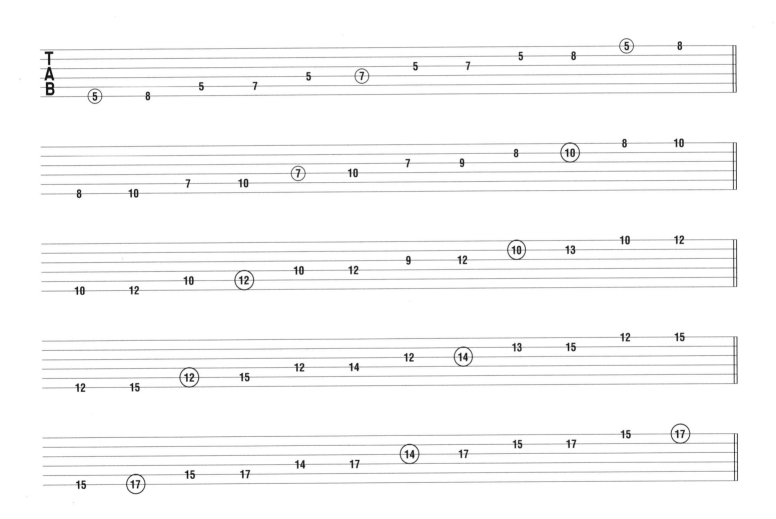

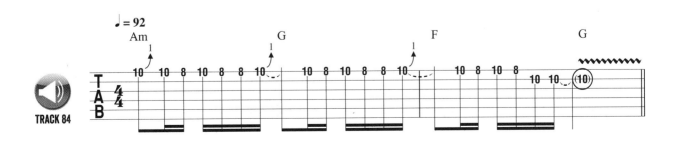

# A#/B♭ MINOR PENTATONIC

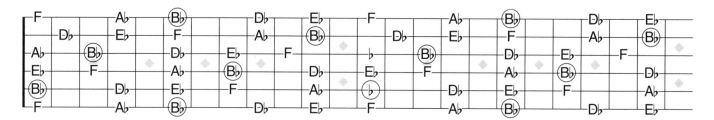

B♭ D♭ E♭ F A♭          1 ♭3 4 5 ♭7

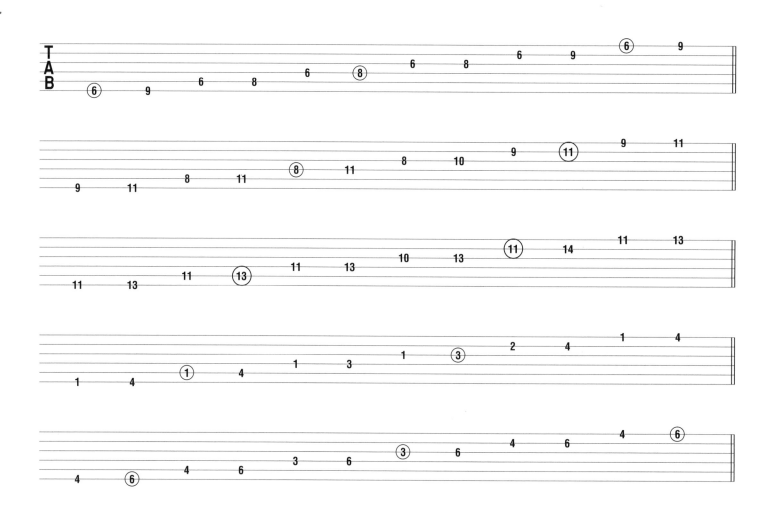

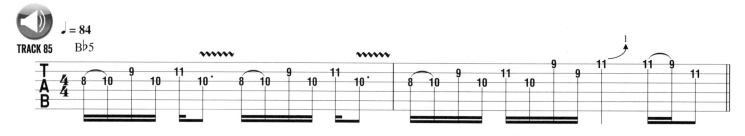

# B MINOR PENTATONIC

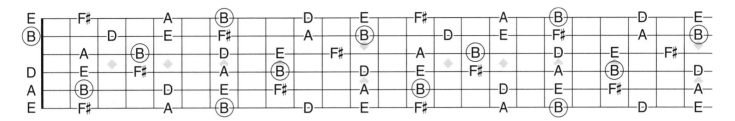

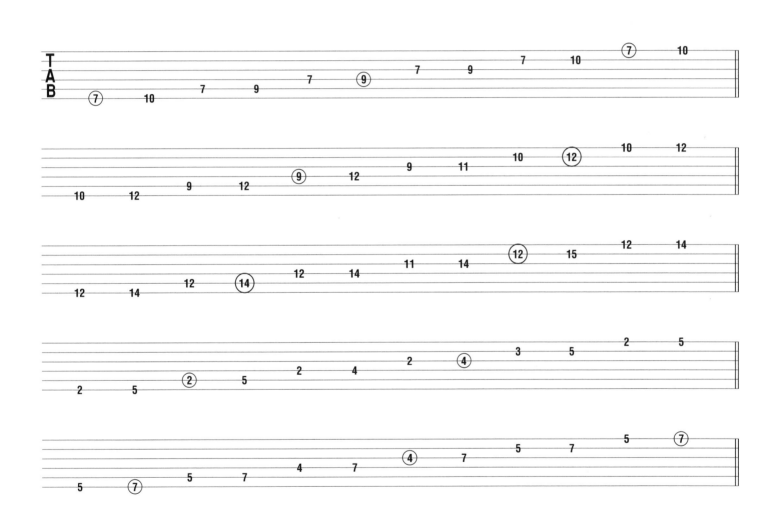

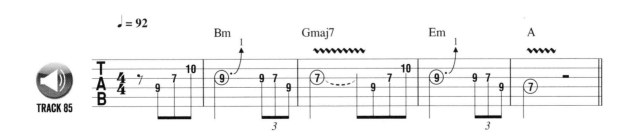

# C MINOR PENTATONIC

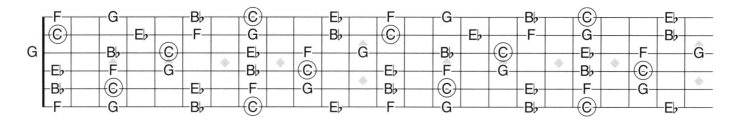

C E♭ F G B♭ 　　1 ♭3 4 5 ♭7

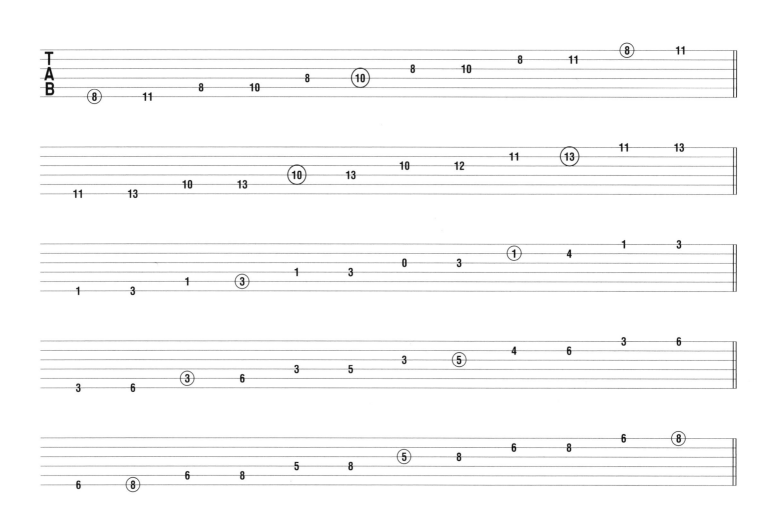

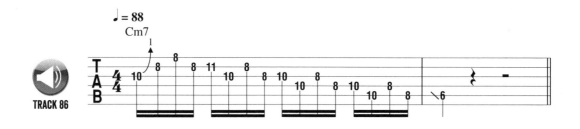

TRACK 86

# C#/Db MINOR PENTATONIC

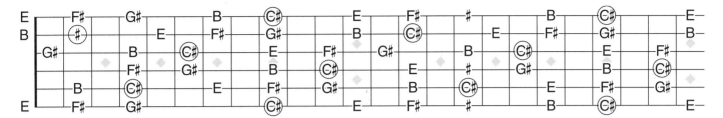

C# E F# G# B          1 b3 4 5 b7

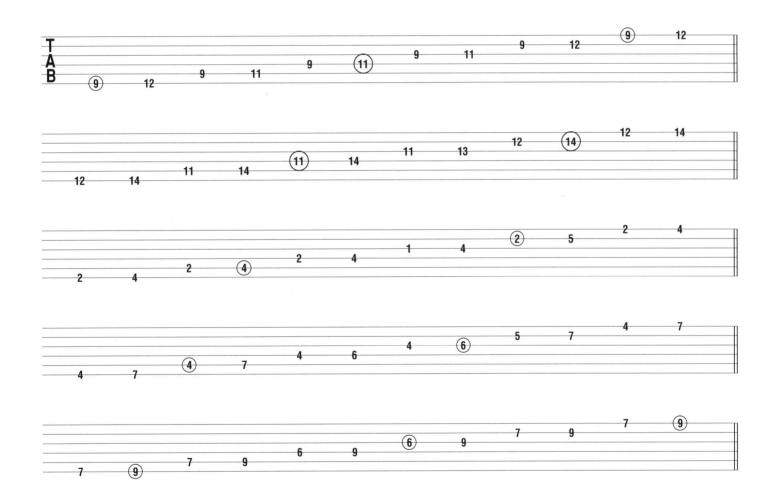

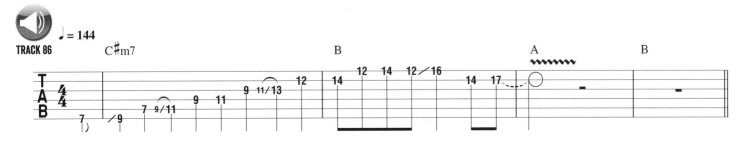

TRACK 86          ♩ = 144

# D MINOR PENTATONIC

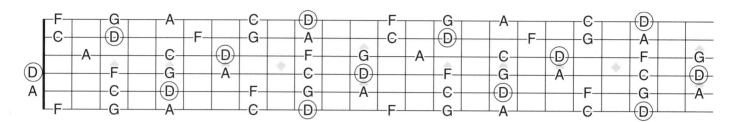

D F G A C      1 ♭3 4 5 ♭7

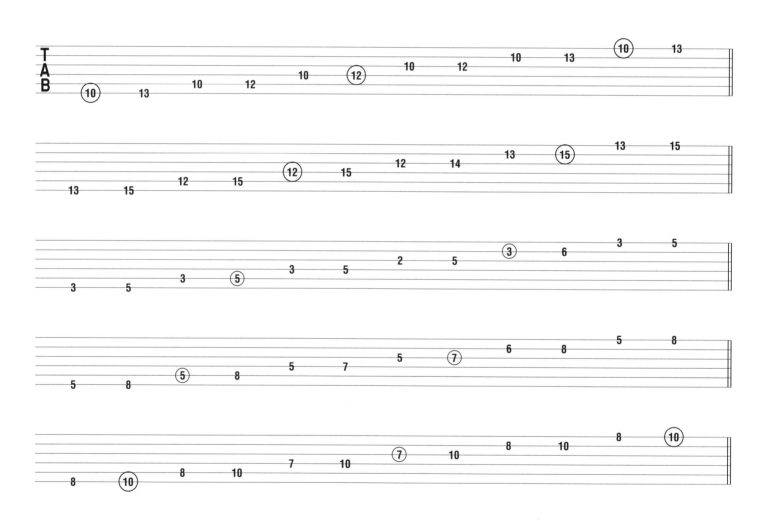

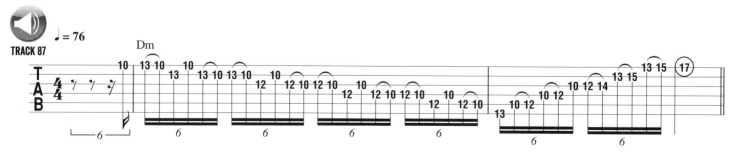

# D#/Eb MINOR PENTATONIC

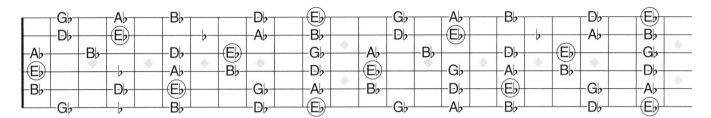

Eb Gb Ab Bb Db          1 b3 4 5 b7

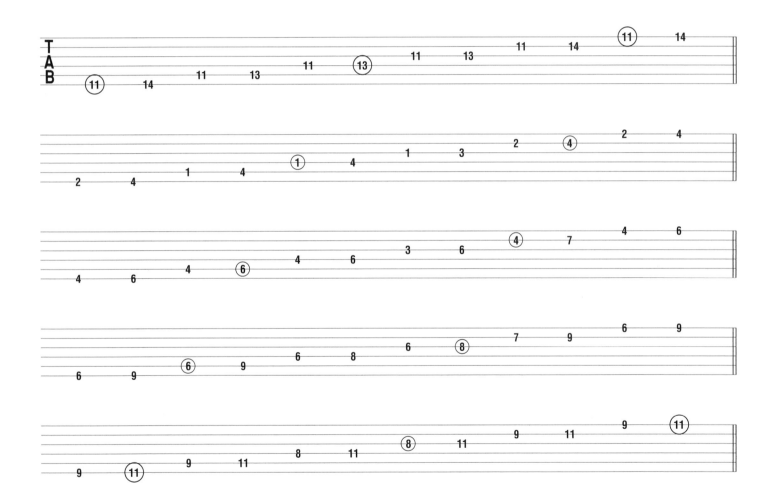

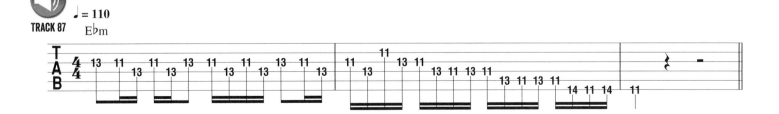

TRACK 87    ♩ = 110
Ebm

# E BLUES

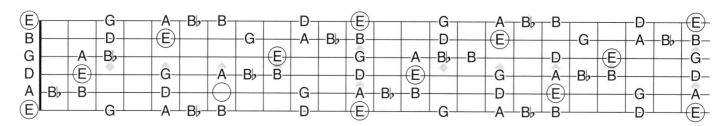

E G A B♭ B D          1 ♭3 4 ♭5 5 ♭7

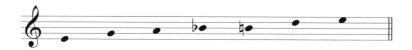

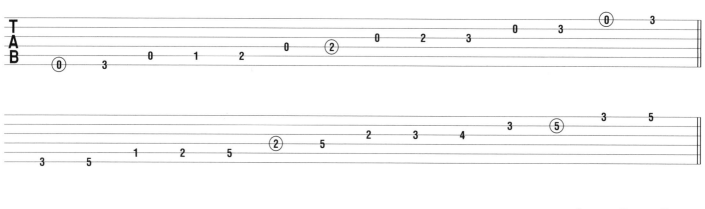

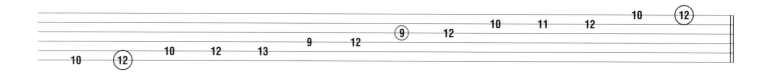

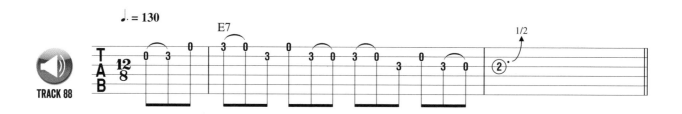

110

# F BLUES

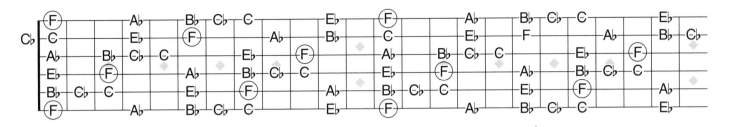

F A♭ B♭ C♭ C E♭        1 ♭3 4 ♭5 5 ♭7

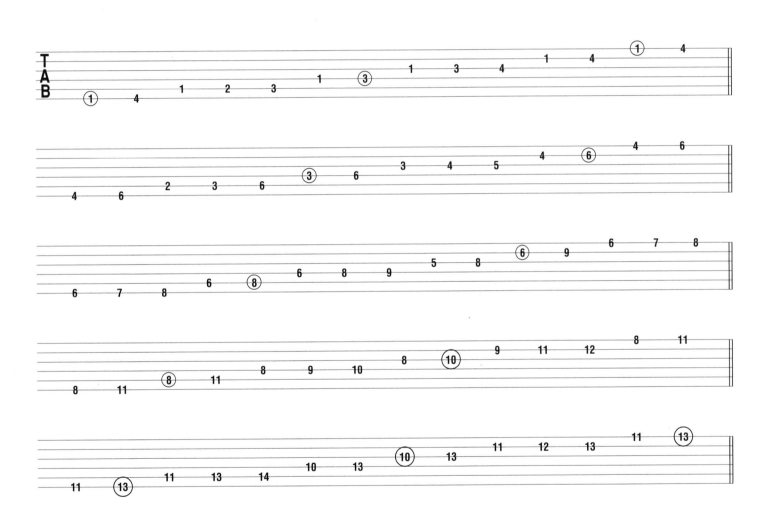

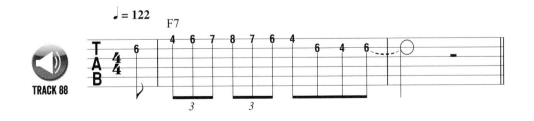

# F#/Gb BLUES

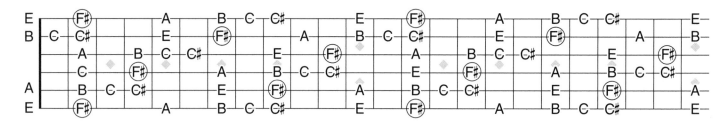

F# A B C C# E          1 ♭3 4 ♭5 5 ♭7

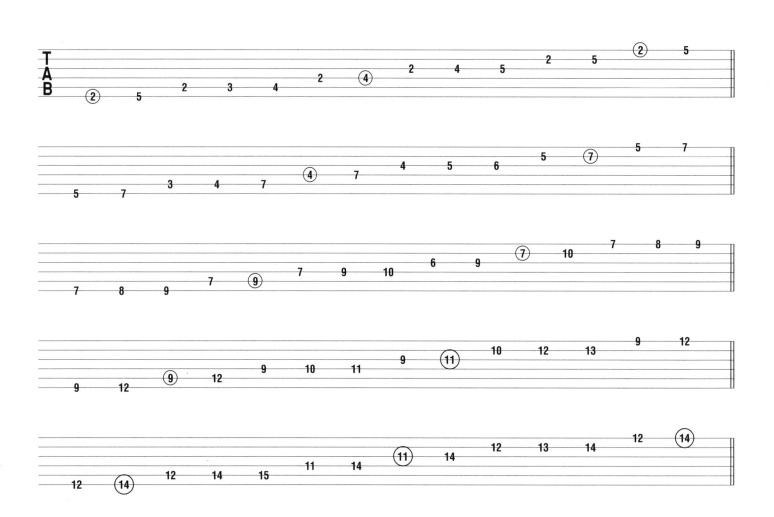

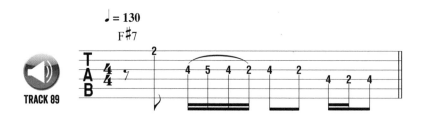

# G BLUES

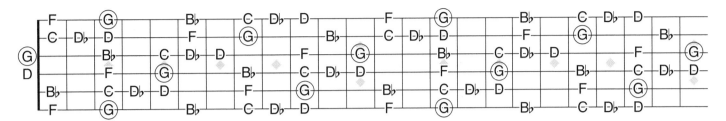

G B♭ C D♭ D F      1 ♭3 4 ♭5 5 ♭7

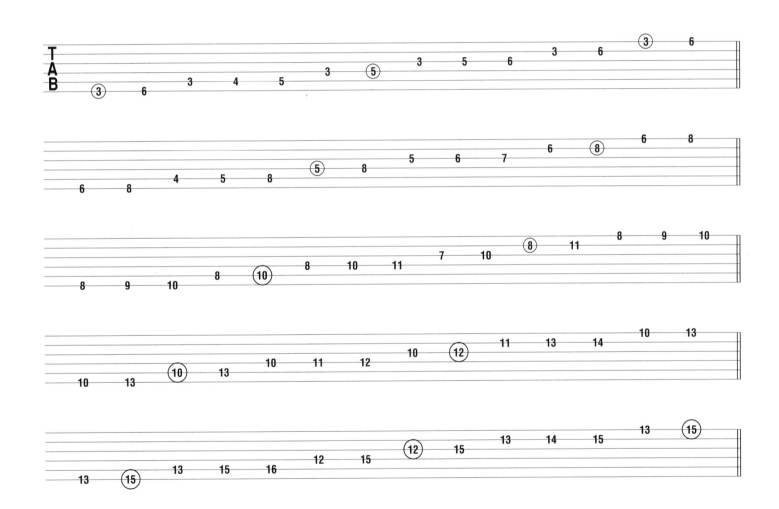

♩ = 130

**TRACK 89**    G7

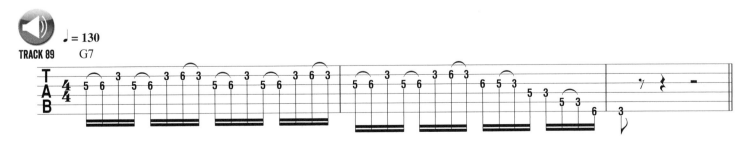

# G#/Ab BLUES

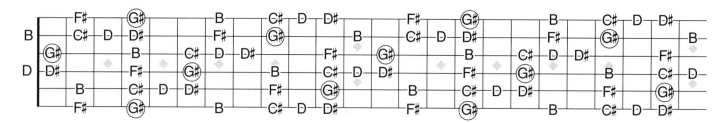

G# B C# D D# F#        1 b3 4 b5 5 b7

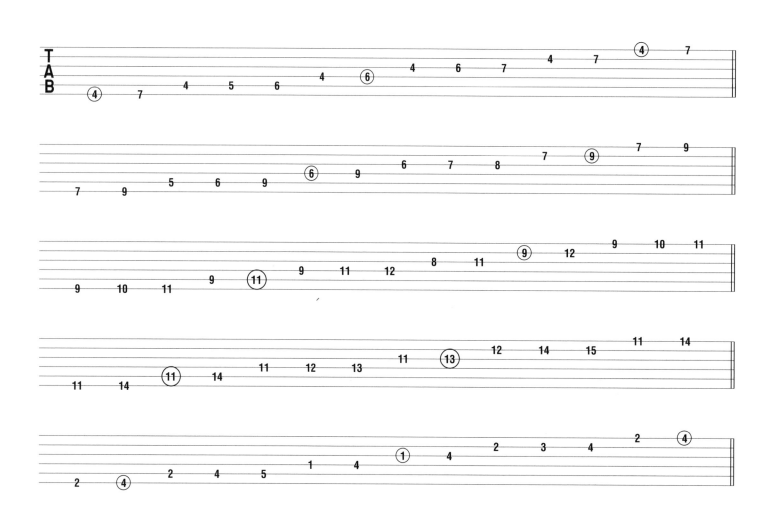

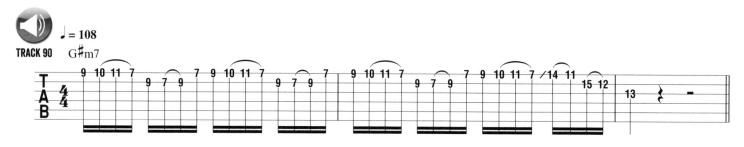

TRACK 90    G#m7    ♩ = 108

# A BLUES

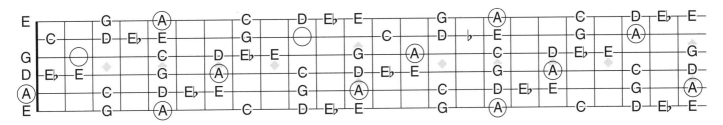

A C D E♭ E G          1 ♭3 4 ♭5 5 ♭7

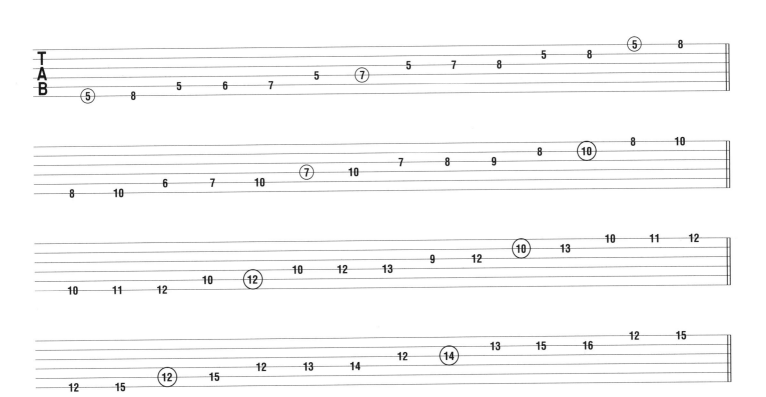

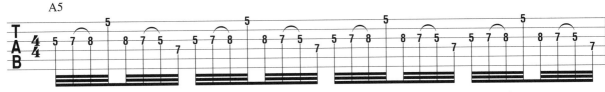

♩ = 60

A5

TRACK 90

# A#/B♭ BLUES

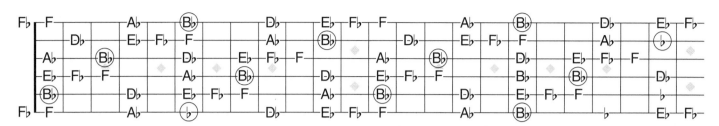

B♭ D♭ E♭ F♭ F A♭          1 ♭3 4 ♭5 5 ♭7

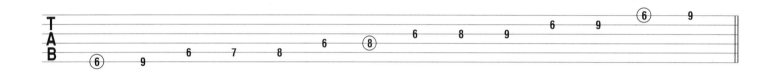

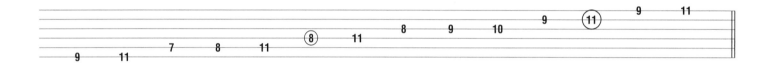

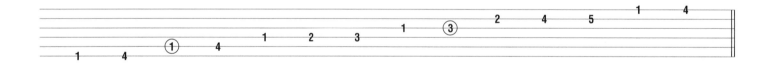

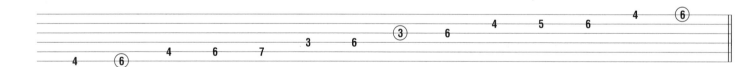

♩ = 105

TRACK 91

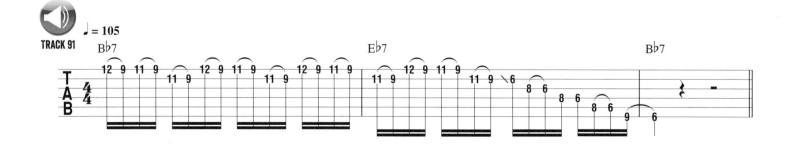

# B BLUES

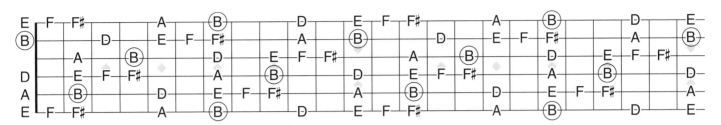

B D E F F# A          1 b3 4 b5 5 b7

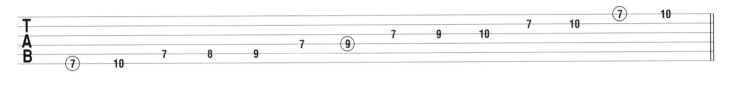

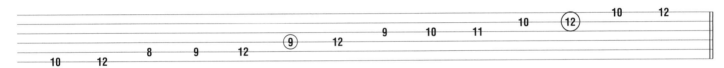

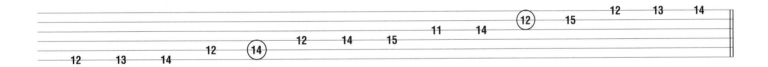

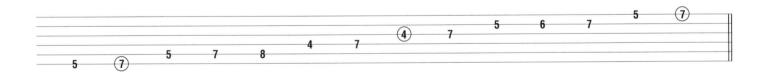

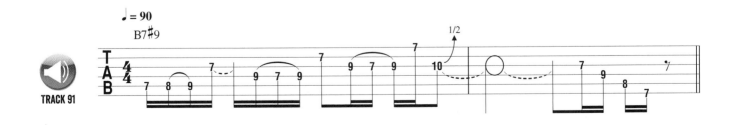

TRACK 91

# C BLUES

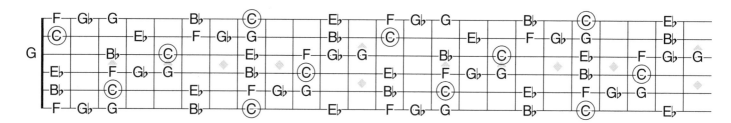

C E♭ F G♭ G B♭        1 ♭3 4 ♭5 5 ♭7

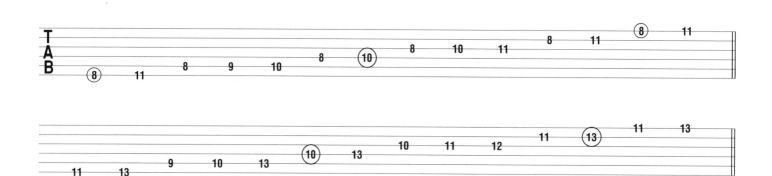

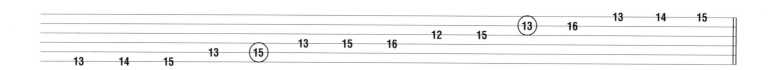

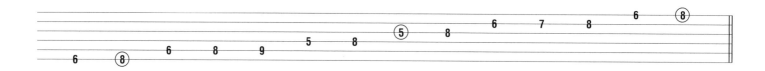

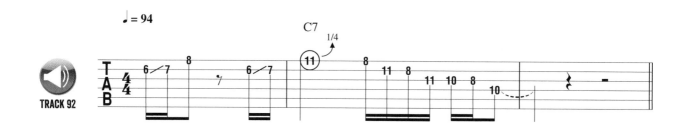

# C#/Db BLUES

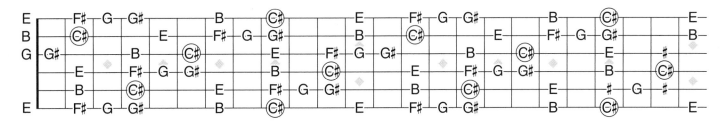

C# E F# G G# B          1 ♭3 4 ♭5 5 ♭7

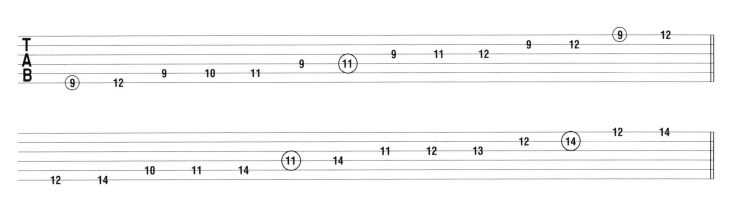

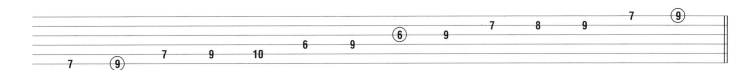

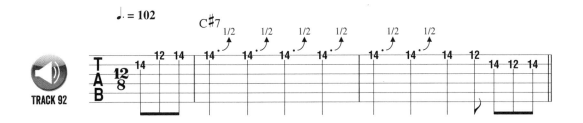

TRACK 92

# D BLUES

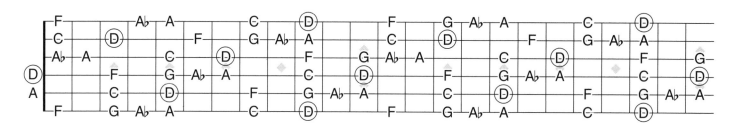

D F G A♭ A C          1 ♭3 4 ♭5 5 ♭7

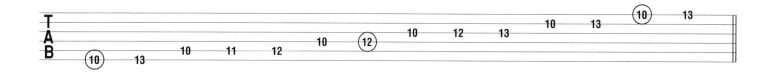

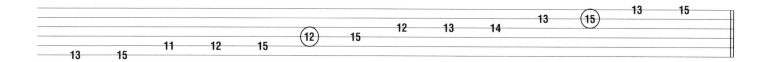

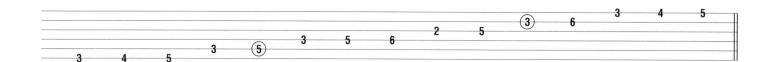

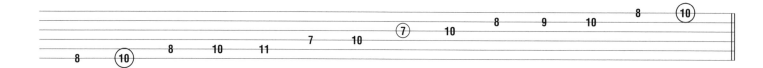

♩ = 138

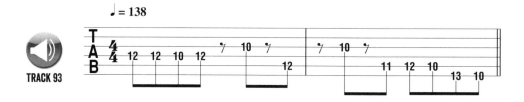

TRACK 93

# D#/Eb BLUES

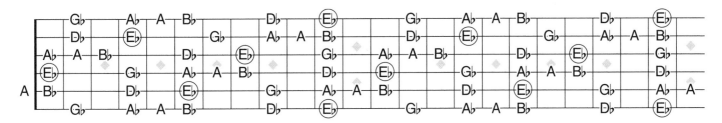

Eb Gb Ab A Bb Db        1 b3 4 b5 5 b7

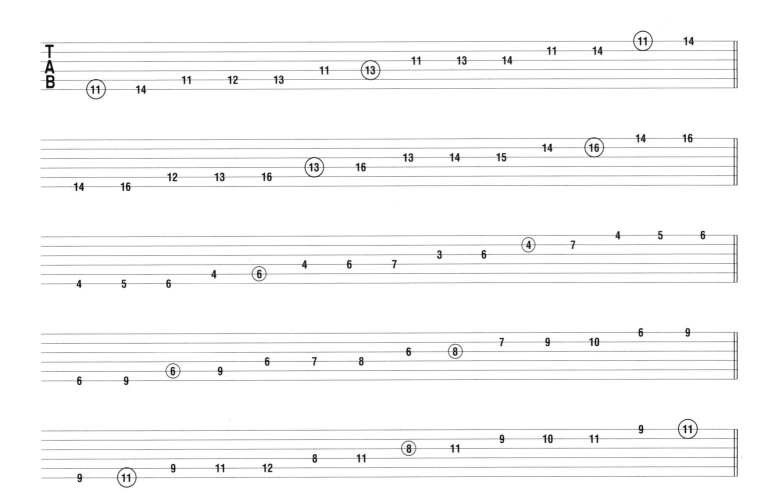

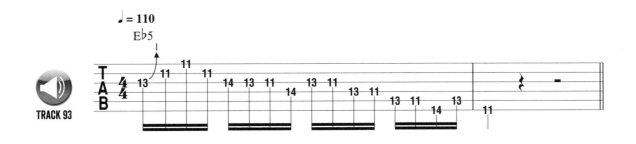

# E MAJOR PENTATONIC

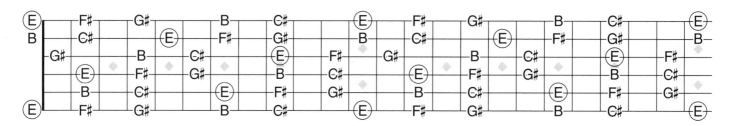

E F# G# B C#          1 2 3 5 6

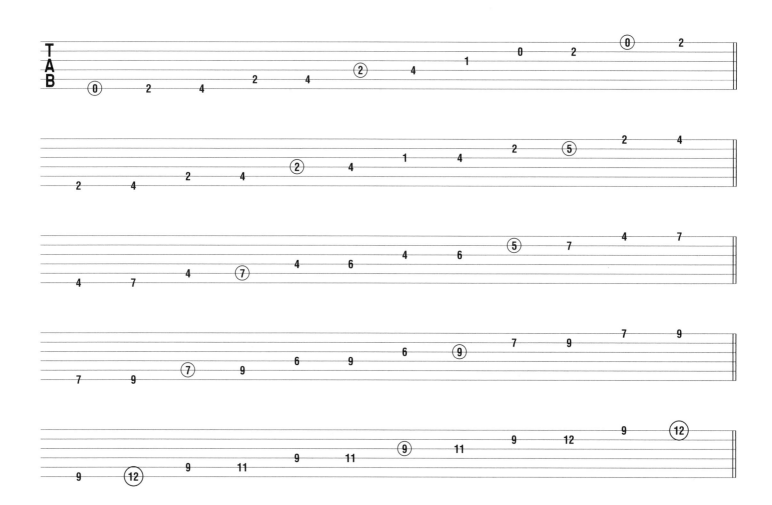

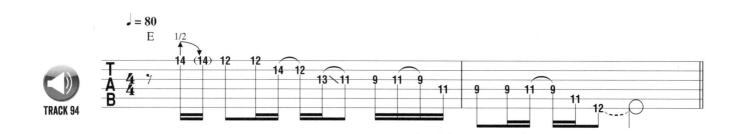

# F MAJOR PENTATONIC

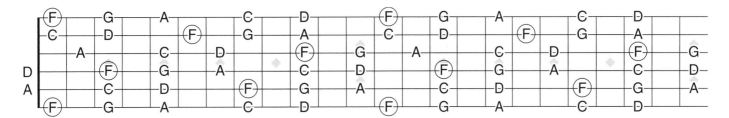

F G A C D          1 2 3 5 6

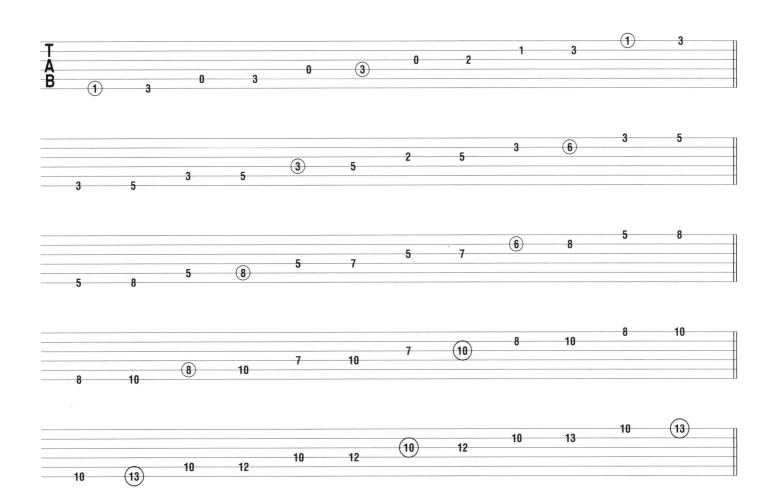

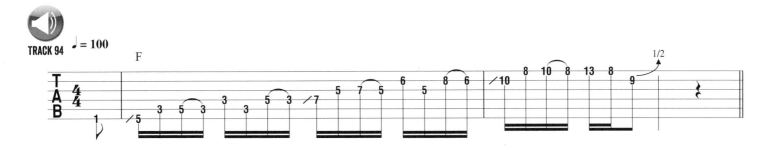

TRACK 94  ♩ = 100

# F#/G♭ MAJOR PENTATONIC

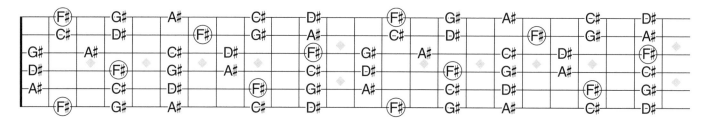

F♯ G♯ A♯ C♯ D♯          1 2 3 5 6

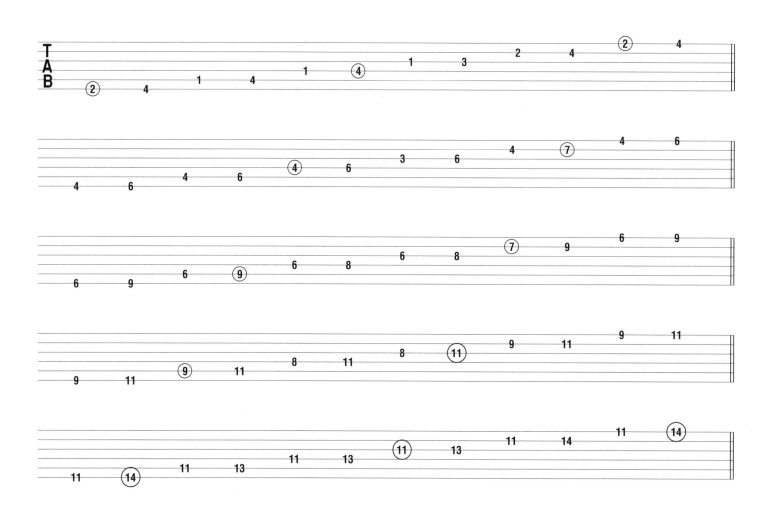

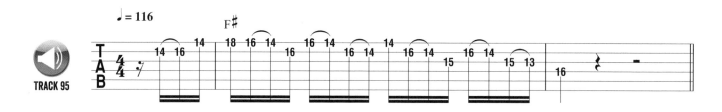

# G MAJOR PENTATONIC

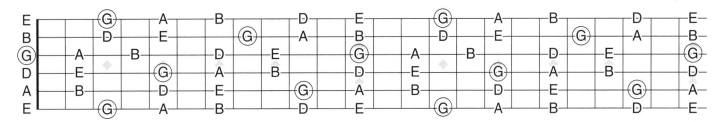

G A B D E          1 2 3 5 6

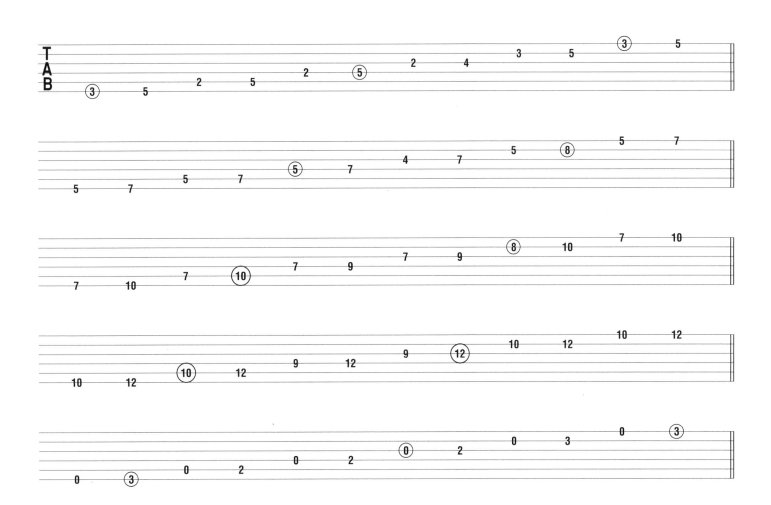

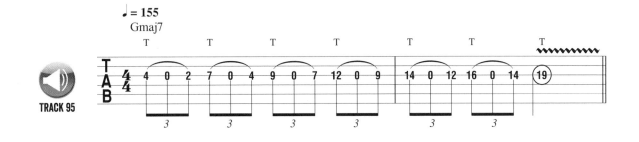

TRACK 95

# G#/A♭ MAJOR PENTATONIC

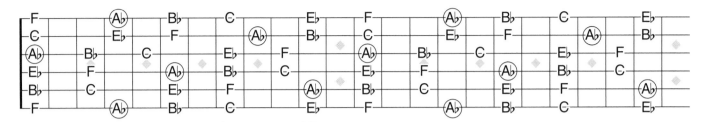

A♭ B♭ C E♭ F        1 2 3 5 6

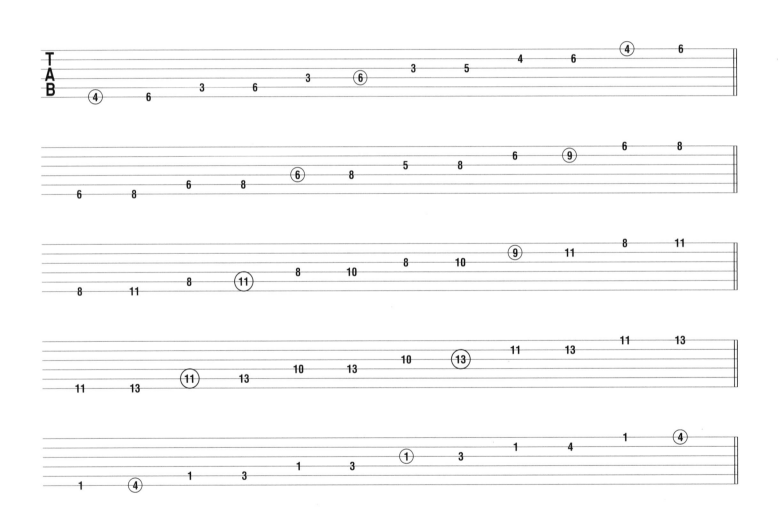

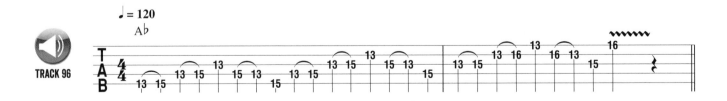

# A MAJOR PENTATONIC

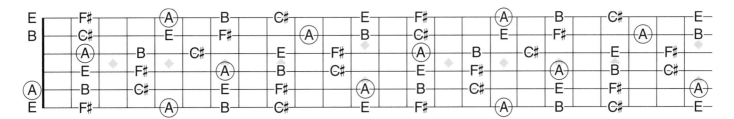

A B C# E F#          1 2 3 5 6

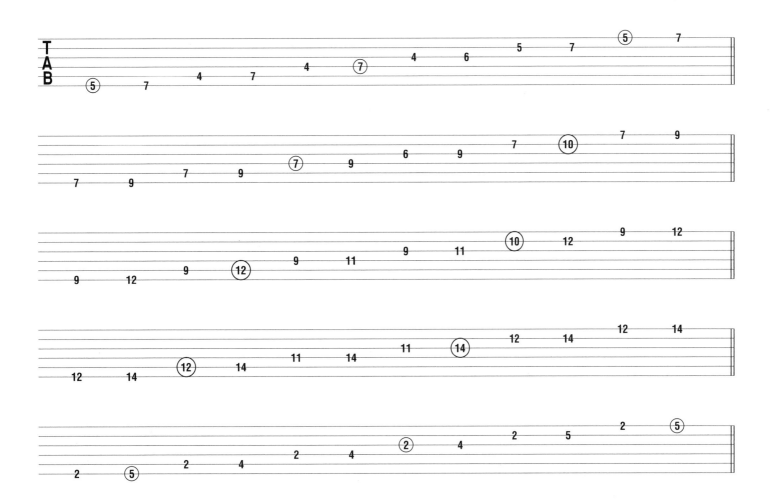

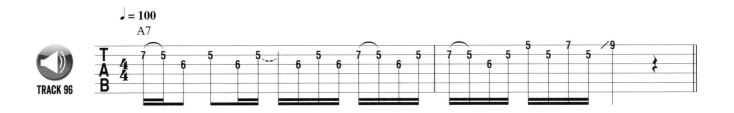

# A#/B♭ MAJOR PENTATONIC

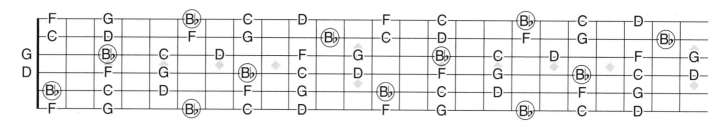

B♭ C D F G          1 2 3 5 6

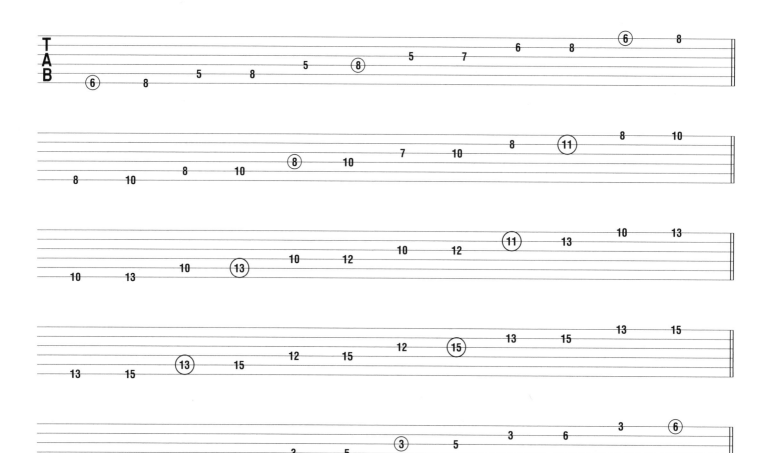

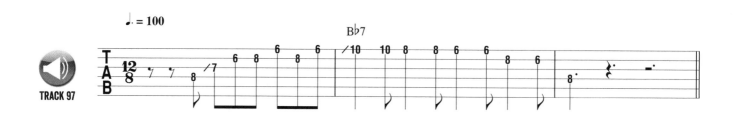

**TRACK 97**

# B MAJOR PENTATONIC

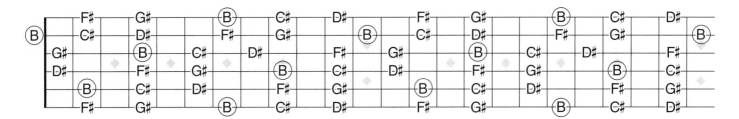

B C# D# F# G#          1 2 3 5 6

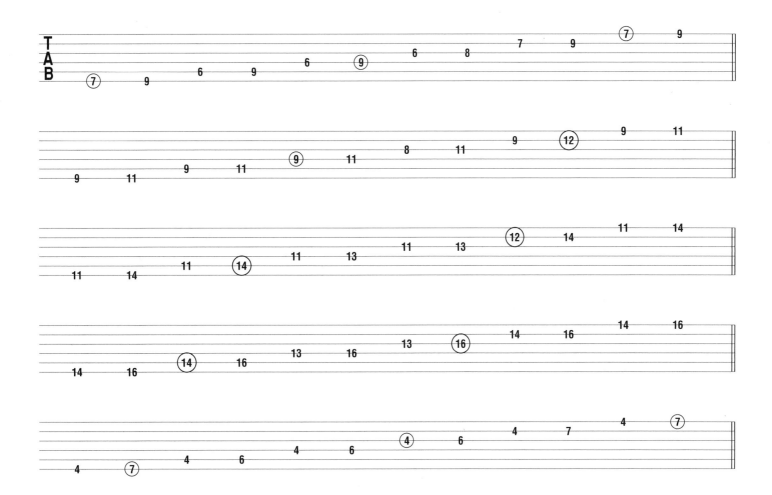

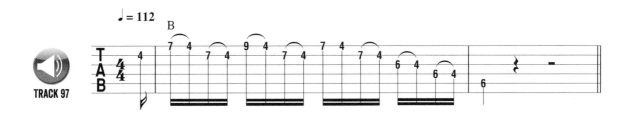

TRACK 97

# C MAJOR PENTATONIC

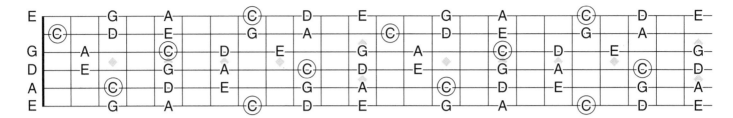

C D E G A        1 2 3 5 6

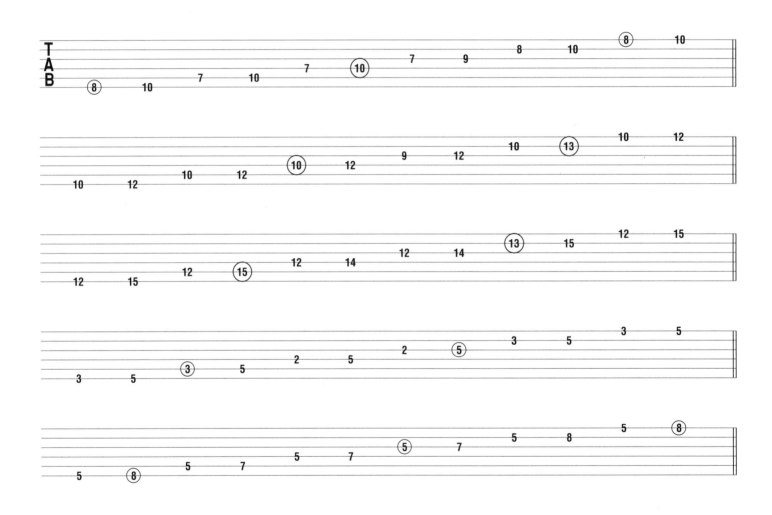

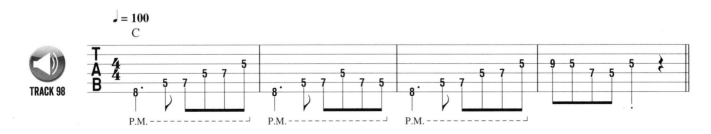

# C#/Db MAJOR PENTATONIC

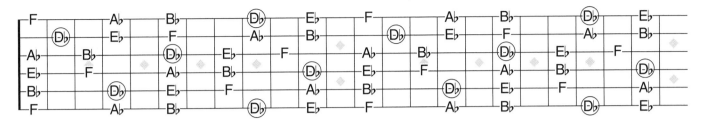

Db Eb F Ab Bb          1 2 3 5 6

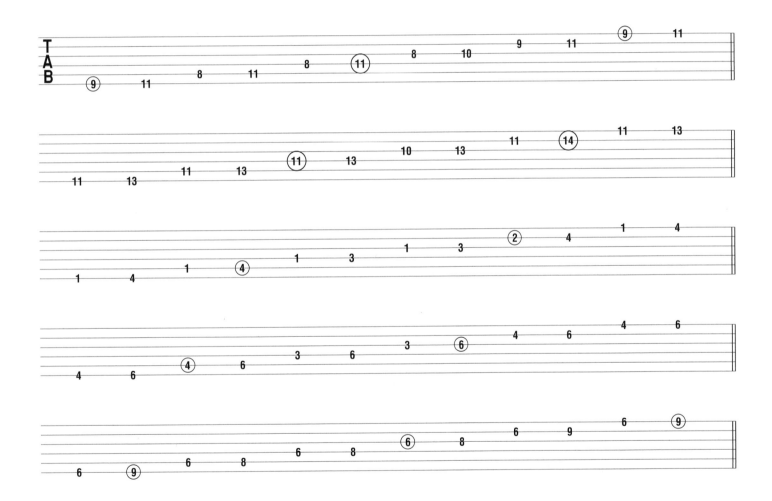

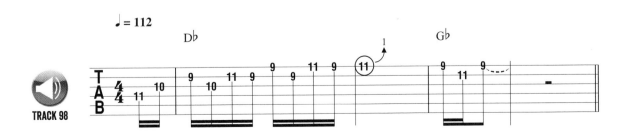

# D MAJOR PENTATONIC

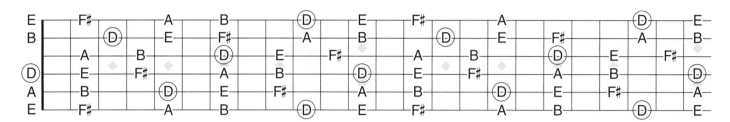

D E F# A B        1 2 3 5 6

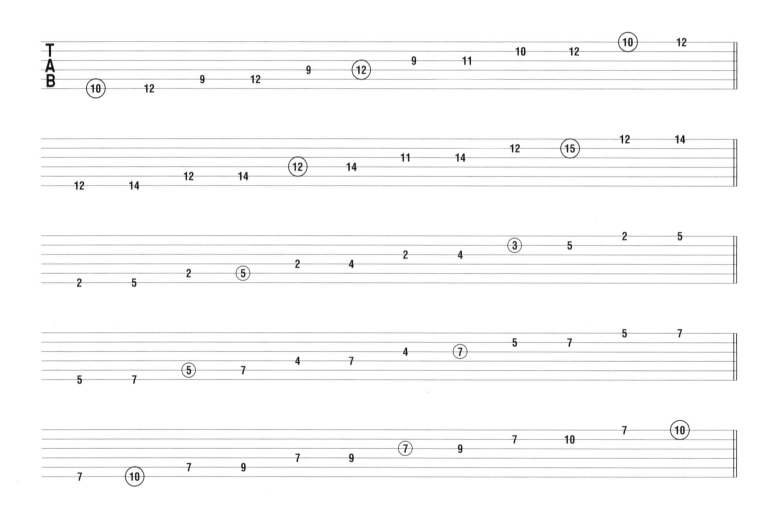

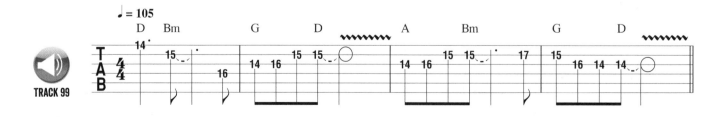

TRACK 99

# D#/E♭ MAJOR PENTATONIC

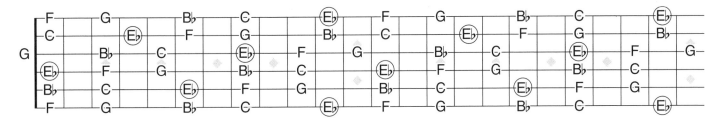

E♭ F G B♭ C          1 2 3 5 6

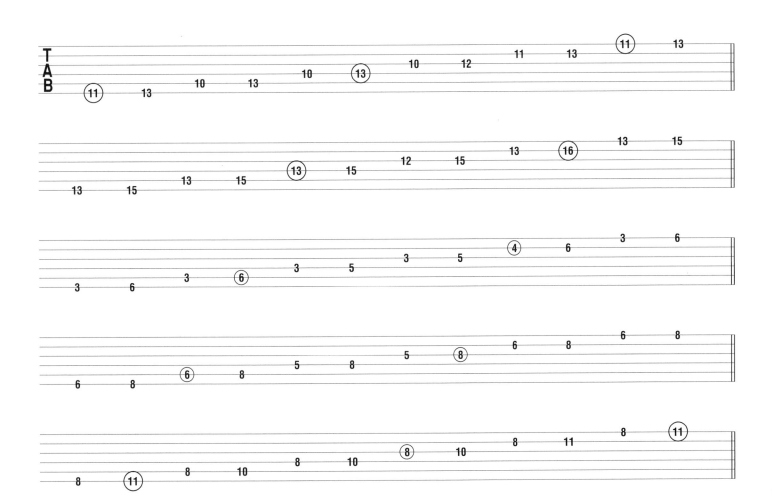

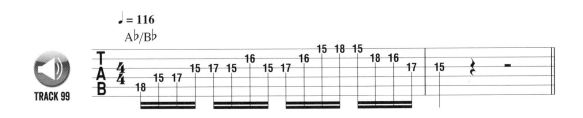

♩ = 116

A♭/B♭

TRACK 99

# ADDITIONAL SCALES

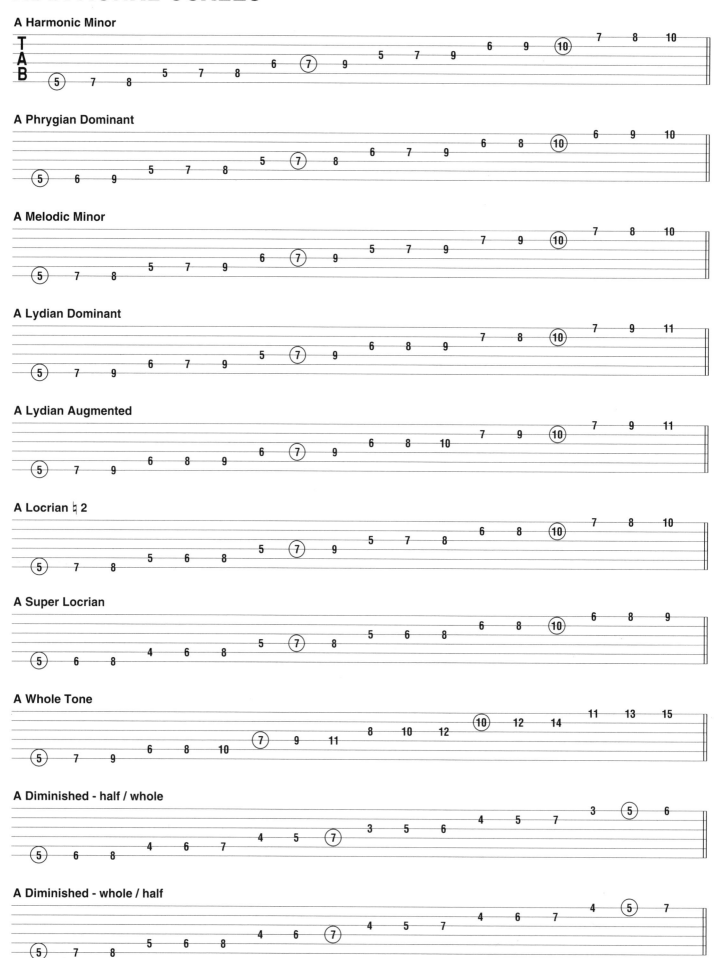

**A Harmonic Minor**

**A Phrygian Dominant**

**A Melodic Minor**

**A Lydian Dominant**

**A Lydian Augmented**

**A Locrian ♮2**

**A Super Locrian**

**A Whole Tone**

**A Diminished - half / whole**

**A Diminished - whole / half**

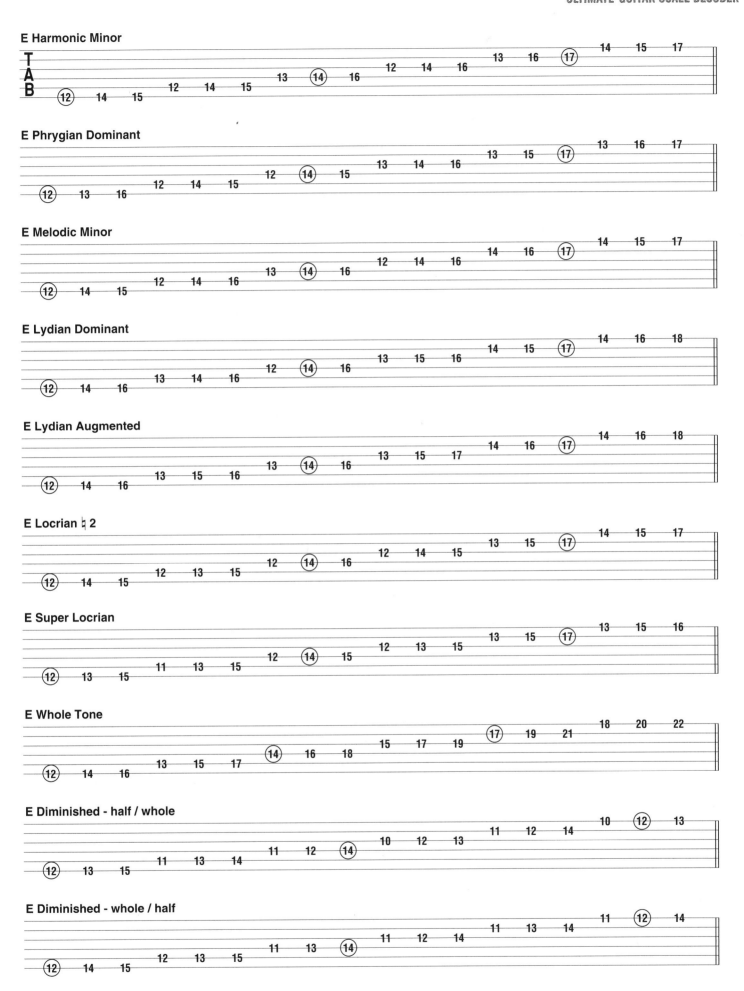

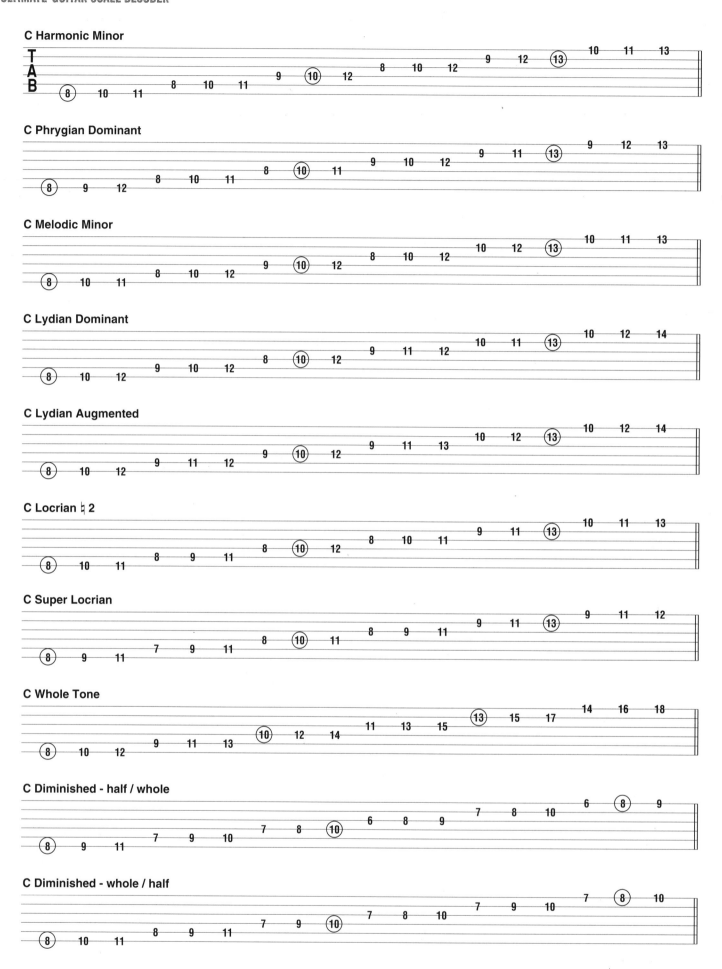